Wisdom of the Dolphins

*Discovering the Mystery
of the
Holographic Universe*

Ilona Selke

©2005 Ilona Selke and Don Paris Ph.D.
First published 1997 by
Living From Vision
Stanwood, WA 98292

All rights reserved. No part of this book may be reproduced or utilized in any form or by any means, electronic or mechanical, without permission in writing from the publisher.

First printed, Feb. 1997 under the title:
"Journey to the Center of Creation" in the USA

Cover Painting, "Playmates" ©Scott Thom published by
Visionary Publishing
Cover design: Don Paris Ph.D.
Petroglyphs: Beverly Vance

Living From Vision®
is a Registered Trade Mark of Allied Forces, Inc.

Selke, Ilona
Wisdom of the Dolphins
Discovering the Mystery of the Holographic Universe

1. Personal Growth
2. Inspirational
I. Title II. Selke, Ilona
ISBN 1-439271-28-3
ISBN 978-1-439271-28-5

A word from the publisher.

After reading the manuscript to *Journey to the Center of Creation* one reviewer sent the following note. We want to pass it along to you, the reader, since it summarizes the intent of the book so well. We hope this book will provide this kind of inspiration to you as well.

Dear Reader,

The concepts in this book are nothing less than earth-shattering.

Ilona Selke has not only traveled merely from Afghanistan to Germany to the United States, but to dimensions beyond the ordinary world we usually think of as "reality."

These realms we often consider imaginary. But what if you suddenly found a tool by which to make your imagination real and receive positive proof of it in the physical world around you, proof that your thoughts do communicate and literally can change historical events.

The world around you is like a magnetic fluid, responsive to the thoughts and feelings within you. This is the story of that kind of imaging, the kind we often do unconsciously, the kind that will change the world entirely by the time you finish reading this book.

A.H. Seattle, WA

Ilona Selke

Dedication

I dedicate this book to the Spark of God in each of us, which is the very force that makes miracles possible.

Acknowledgments

I would like to give thanks to all the beings that have helped co-create this book. Foremost, I give my deepest thanks to the dolphins, angels, and inter-dimensional beings for their help and for the miracles that have resulted from their help.

Additionally, many people have contributed to the ideas and methods presented in this story. I appreciate each of you very much from the depth of my heart, as anything we individually create is never created alone.

With deep gratitude I thank my Beloved, Don Paris for your Love, for all the incredible wisdom and light, the endless hours of help and editing, the willingness to go on adventures together—both inner and outer—and the ability to bring out the best in each person. I thank my mother Ingeborg Selke for her wisdom and ability to see into the depth of my soul, and who believed in me; my father who died but helped from "the other side" since I was a toddler; my sister, Marion Selke, who sees the best in me and is an incredible artist; and my niece, Lena, who is an angel.

I thank Dr. Vernon Wolf, developer of Holodynamics, for bringing a great method to the public; Dr. Rod Newton for a sustained vision and tools for a better world; all the "crazy" scientists who are daring enough to stick their necks out; John Lilly for all the dolphin research and for keeping his promise to the dolphins; and Roberta Quist-

Goodman for her dolphin wisdom and stories that inspire and provide hope for humanity.

Thanks to Loraine for her dolphin love and inspiration; to Terry Walker for helping me in the waves and being in the buddy system; Carl for his beautiful light in Hawaii; Fatah for sending his true Aloha Spirit to us in the midst of all the bustle; Beverly Vance for the nice line art, Scott Thom for the beautiful painting on the front cover, Angelika Hansen and Trisha Lamb Feuerstein for their kind editing and support; Al Harris for his support in vision and proofing; Bobbie Barnes for putting the methods to successful test with at-risk students; Dorothy Miller, our office angel; and Sharry Edwards for her incredible research on Sound and Healing.

Special thanks to all the students and teachers of the course "Living From Vision™" in Germany and America, whose magical life transformations gave me the energy and impetus to get the message out to many more people; all my friends, unnamed as they may be, whose love and support makes life worth living; all the dolphin-book authors for inspiration; and Spirit, which makes Life a miracle.

Prologue

As the human race, we stand at a crossroads. We have the option of making the necessary evolutionary adjustments and survive as a race, or not make them and perish. For the last ten thousand years we have developed our rational mind to such an extent that we have become rather powerful in some ways. Yet, just as we stand at the brink of bringing on self-destruction because of our rational ability, many humans are starting to feel a yearning for a deeper knowledge, one that comes from the depth of our souls.

We sense this wisdom and hear about it in tales from ancient people, the ones who lived in harmony with nature, closer to the world of dreaming. We hear of people who say that their dreams hold our world together. What will happen when they are gone, when the last of the old ones have been driven out of our world and have taken with them the knowledge of dreaming the world into being? Will we find out that they knew something we will need for our continued existence?

The need for us to wake up and remember is growing each day. If we keep separating ourselves from the dreams we create by using our logical mind only, we humans may not survive much longer.

Yet, in the midst of us are beings who are remembering, ancient ones who are awakening every day. There are teachers who don't obviously teach but who invite any of us who can sense our own potential to reawaken to what lies hidden within us.

Dolphins have proved to be such teachers to me, and they seem to talk to many of us in our hearts. An old memory is resurfacing that dolphins are the angels of our dimension and that they are here to help us reconnect with our inherent knowledge that the world is an intricate fabric of dreams. We are here to help co-create our dream of humanity, if we could but remember to shift from solely rational living to realizing the power of our ancient mind, our inner vision.

The fabric of life awaits our reentry into an active role of living wisdom. How can we integrate the ancient wisdom into our daily lives, when we are so urbanized, so governed by a rational world?

The Wisdom of the Dolphins chronicles such a possibility and shows how we can invite "coincidences," eventually seeing living proof of our dreams come true. It is my hope to inspire you to become a dreamer in the new dream of humanity.

1

The warm ocean water surrounded me like a blanket. Crystal clear, turquoise water expanded into quiet depths beneath me. Light rays flowed past my body in long streaks, creating a surreal feeling in this still, underwater world. Only the steady sound of my breath through the snorkel gave my human ears something familiar to hold on to.

Don, my Beloved, and I were swimming with a dear woman friend in a bay known for its calm water and the possibility of encountering dolphins.

Suddenly, out of the blue, I saw their shadowy outline beneath me in the water. In groups of two, three, and more, an entire pod of dolphins came swimming my way.

For years I had been experimenting with sending images to the dolphins. When I entered the water today, I began visualizing myself swimming with one dolphin on each side of me, as though I were being taken on a tour. I was hoping that they would hear my prayers and be with me. And here they were!

I took a deep breath and dived into the depths of the ocean, then veered off to one side, letting the dolphins know that I knew at least *some* underwater social etiquette. To my great surprise, one dolphin swam up to my side and made eye contact with me. Trying to keep my excitement contained, I kept pace with the dolphin as we spiraled underwater, keeping our eyes locked on one another. Three other dolphins ascended from below us, coming up to breathe, and we surfaced together as I caught my breath. As quickly as possible, I dived down again. The three dolphins had swooped back down and were now swimming slightly beneath me.

Suddenly something strange started happening to me. I felt like I was gliding underwater and didn't seem to need air. As though I were part of a pod with the three dolphins beneath me, I felt like I was in tow, enveloped in a ball of energy. We became one, belonging together. The immense silence of the ocean engulfed me, and I felt suspended in another kind of reality. I was gliding in an envelope of oneness with these three dolphins. For a moment in time there was no separation between being human and being dolphin. My human weakness was altered, my need to breathe suspended for a time.

The joy of this moment was all I perceived and cared about. Gone were thoughts of yesterday or tomorrow. A wave of gratefulness filled my entire heart and mind. After what seemed like an eternity, I eventually came up for air.

What had happened? Had the water and the dolphins altered my perception so much that I thought I was underwater longer than I actually had been? How could I know?

As I was pondering these questions, Don came into view just as he dived down in perfect timing with several dolphins. Turning upside down, one dolphin showed her white belly to Don, much like dolphins do when they swim with each other. Don looked sleek underwater in his wetsuit, gliding in synchronous movements with this small group. I kept watching in amazement at the sheer grace of the dolphins and their apparent willingness to take us humans into their pod.

Wisdom of the Dolphins

After watching Don for a while, I became a little nervous. Wasn't it time for him to come up for air? He was probably thirty feet down and still had to allow for enough air to return to the surface. I grew more and more anxious. Our friend also saw Don and felt almost like she was suffocating herself just watching him. But Don stayed in sync and swam along with the pod. Eventually he came up to breathe, together with the three dolphins, long after we, the ones watching, had run out of air.

Don was exhilarated! He had been aware of not needing to breathe. The dolphins mentally told him to go get air, as though they knew his physical limits, and then accompanied him to the surface!

With great excitement Don told us of his previous experience. Two dolphins had flanked him and accompanied him closer to shore, where they showed him their underwater garden. For twenty minutes they gave him a tour, staying close and seemingly attempting to show him something of value. The feeling was indescribable, and Don's glowing eyes and exuberant energy hinted at the ecstatic joy he had felt in the presence of the dolphins.

Why did Don have the exact experience I had envisioned for myself, and why did it happen to him instead of me?

I had become accustomed to the fact that "as you imagine, so it will be." On this day I had envisioned an experience for myself, which in all the years of being with the dolphins had never happened to me before. I had learned by experience that dolphins seem to read our minds and respond to the images we hold inside, but this day Don had the very experience I had imagined and hoped to have myself.

Trying not to be envious of his experience, I wondered about it as I floated like a cork on the surface of the ocean. I was relaxing and catching my breath before we started our long swim back to shore. The dolphins had performed an action in which I had envisioned myself participating. Just how did they mix up Don and me? Had they gotten the right image and acted on it, but missed the target?

Suddenly it dawned on me. I heard the question in my mind, "Aren't you understanding yourself and Don to be One?" Of course we are, I realized! Don and I are intrinsically paired, and what one experiences can be almost as real to the other.

Dolphins may not experience the boundaries between individuals as distinctly as humans do. Dolphins feel each other's feelings much more strongly, and at least for wild dolphins, empathy seems much more developed. In this light, I was thrilled for Don to have had the experience I had envisioned for myself. I was willing to open my heart to receive the full joy of the experience the dolphins brought to him and vicariously to me.

This was yet another lesson I learned from the dolphins. The journey up to this point had been adventurous and exciting and got better with each new step. I had been learning that the images we hold and live by influence our personal lives. After I had sufficiently learned to use these processes in my own life, the dolphins asked me to help them in their fight for survival. Helping them as best I could, I discovered the miracle of how interwoven our imagination and our universe really is.

But what a journey it had been to arrive at this understanding! I thought of our first trip to Hawaii.

2

We were milling about the San Francisco Airport shortly before boarding the plane to Kauai, one of the lushest islands of Hawaii. Months of growing excitement had passed with dreams of things to come and hopes of entering a new world. The mysterious world of dolphins had captured our hearts, and we were about to enter into a reality hitherto unknown to us.

"Ladies and gentlemen, flight number 258 to Honolulu has been delayed until further notice due to a technical problem. We hope to be departing in a few hours." The voice coming through the loudspeakers broke my reverie. A groan filled the air around us. I slowly opened my eyes to meet the gentle gaze of Don, who also had been absorbed in his inner world. How did we get this lucky? Blue luminous light shone forth from his inner being, sensing my every thought and feeling. Enveloped by a knowingness, we often communicated telepathically. "Did we like what we just heard?" we wondered simultaneously.

Don said playfully, "Oops, I think we are in the wrong universe; this will put us into Honolulu by late evening, and we will miss our connection to Kauai."

I agreed by nodding and added, "Let's switch into another universe."

We had been reading and hearing about new ideas from quantum physics. Instead of there being only a single reality, it had been postulated that innumerable realities existed in parallel to one another. Many possible universes were thought to be existing all at once in the same space, separated only by frequencies. But this new worldview was not yet popular knowledge.

The old worldview of a clockwork universe was Newton's idea. This world functioned predictably, in an orderly manner, and was independent of any thoughts, feelings, or consciousness. This orderly, mechanical view of the universe had its price however. Manipulating the wheels of the clock was all the excitement that was left for the human race. The results of this manipulation of nature are visible everywhere and the level of destruction has reached a dangerous degree, threatening our very survival.

All this humans have "achieved" by organizing their understanding of the universe in a mechanical manner, and what a price we have paid! Most people have learned to believe that they are simply a wheel in the machine and that what they think does not matter much.

The Newtonian view of the universe has ultimately proved to be more than boring. It is outright devoid of the possibility of adventure and is showing signs of endangering the very life upon which we depend.

Quantum physics however has begun to change all that. It was hypothesized that an observing consciousness, in other words a being with awareness, is an integral factor in making the universe tick. It is the torchlight of attention that gives shape to the many possibilities of manifestation. And it is attention which can bring about the manifestation of one of the many parallel universes.

An experiment finally put an end to a hypothesis which had plagued the scientific world during Einstein's lifetime. Originally, Einstein, Podolsky and Rosen postulated that light was traveling at the absolute limit in the physical universe. But in 1985, an experiment at College Park, Maryland, was done that proved the exact opposite. It was demonstrated that information travels faster than the speed of light and that photon particles seem to communicate to one other the expectations the scientist was looking for.

Quantum physics is not the only viewpoint that accepts that consciousness interacts with the world around us. It is just a new version of knowledge that seers from all cultures have known and practiced since time immemorial.

As we sat stunned by the announcement of the delayed flight I wondered, "Did this delay have purpose? Was it a test of how well we behaved like sheep, believing ourselves to be the victims of circumstance?"

"OK," Don said, " let's shift into another universe." Both Don and I closed our eyes and began practicing what we had learned.

Sinking deeper into my inner sense of being, I began seeing that everything is interconnected. I was enveloped by what appeared to be liquid light. Everyone around me was part and parcel of why things were the way they happened to be. I moved further up in my inner vision, and saw a larger part of the picture. I approached the level from where we make choices. Here I could choose to be in one of the other possible and parallel realities. More and more luminous light filled my inner vision. Then I saw a snapshot in my mind of how I actually wanted my experience to be: *The airplane is perfect; I see the energy pattern adjusting around the fuselage and the engines. I feel we are in a perfectly timed universe. I am willing to be at ease and fly when the time is right, when it is in harmony with all that is and for the highest purpose of all concerned. Bingo! I can feel it. It is true in my heart. Now.*

    I blinked my eyes open, quickly letting go of all feelings of trying, wanting, or wishing, and I simply noticed my environment.

    All right! I enjoyed being able to choose my universe. Who said that life is what it appears to be? But what learning it had been just to get to this point! How many times did I wince at the doubt-filled thought, "What if I am just pretending?" How many times had the angels shuddered, watching me undo my own miracles in a few seconds of doubt?

    Barely five minutes later another announcement filled the air. "Ladies and gentlemen," a bright voice sounded through the loudspeaker, "we are happy to announce that our technicians were able to locate the problem and repair it. We will begin boarding in a few minutes."

    We jumped up and down. Yeah!! Life is not what it seems! Switching universes. We were getting the hang of it!

3

Happily we got our things together and walked down the aisles of our "new-universe-airplane." It didn't look much different from the other universe in which we would have had to wait for several hours. As a matter of fact, if I hadn't experienced this process so many times before, I easily could have written it all off as coincidence. But I had learned to give up shrugging my shoulders and passing it off as such. That would have given me an easy way out of any responsibility and would always keep me as a spectator in a clockwork universe. Instead I had learned to realize that the fabric of the universe I live in is far more flexible than I ever dreamed possible.

Well, all the people on board seemed to look pretty much the same. I could see why most of present-day humanity looks at the three-dimensional world and concludes that everything behaves according to the laws we learned in school. This viewpoint makes everything appear safe and stable. Stability has its advantages, and some of it is certainly necessary in order to have any semblance of reality, yet I had come to trust in a more nonlinear way of thinking, always proving every step of the way to myself. I had only wanted to accept these new ideas if they proved to be usable for increasing the quality of life for myself and others, if they made sense in day-to-day life, and finally only if they were in alignment with an energy I call Love, God, or the Source.

Moving through the narrow aisle of the airplane, we finally found our seats, stored our bags, and sat down, making ourselves comfortable. Don looked at me with shining eyes, his gaze touching me like a star descended from Heaven, but with a twinkle in his eyes that said "I love living in this magical universe with you."

We held each other's hands and closed our eyes, taking a minute to thank All-that-Is. Breathing with a sense of gratitude, we moved to a quiet place inside. As if we could move through the layers of clouds, we moved higher and higher until we broke through into the luminous sunlight, feeling free, with endless joy around us. We let our sense of Self spread out into the light, let it permeate us, then moved out into it and let the light flood back in. I could sense Don's presence in this field of light permeating mine. "What grace it is to be here!" I thought.

Meanwhile, we rolled onto the airfield and were next in line for takeoff. How my world had changed since the days I worked as a flight attendant for Lufthansa when I was twenty years old! Since then, life had been a continuous movement of growth, requiring me to be continuously real by being truthful with myself and my motivations. I had moved on with the help of human teachers, beings from other dimensions and other species, and discovered greater and greater mysteries. But the cost was sometimes tremendous! To remain loving in the face of denial, to seek understanding instead of needing to be right or purer were real pains to grow through. It was trial and error, and trial again.

"Welcome to our flight to Hawaii! Flight attendants, please prepare for takeoff."

Wisdom of the Dolphins

The captain's voice over the loudspeakers moved me slightly out of my reverie. Soon we were flying past the coast of San Francisco, leaving the land masses behind and climbing closer to the sun. Clouds piled up next to us, but we broke through, and the land of everlasting sunshine was all around us. It is strange how down on earth we often pray for sunshine, even though it is actually always there. The sun's light is continuously shining; only the clouds are between us and the light. And those clouds can be thick sometimes!

4

With a thoughtful sigh I turned in my seat in the airplane, and Don looked at me inquisitively. "Oh, I'm just pondering the meaning of clouds," I said to him smiling, since I knew he would understand. We were flying over the Pacific Ocean by now, and the cloud cover had opened up for some breathtaking views of the cloudscapes beneath us.

"Time must look like that from one perspective," I thought. Once we are above the time horizon we can see the entire timescape. But from within the time picture it all looks sequential and linear. Why have we, as humans, not learned to rise above the time horizon occasionally and take a bigger look at our present situation?

Years earlier Don and I had inwardly and outwardly asked for a time-travel machine. We figured that this would be an exciting way of spending time. We could zoom back and forth between different dimensions of time and space. When we stumbled across the SE-5 we didn't realize the connection at first. The SE-5 is an instrument designed to read and balance subtle information fields. These fields of information surround everything like a blueprint, from living things to "solid" matter.

Using this kind of instrumentation, tests were done for the USDA to show how bugs were driven away from cornfields in the 1950s without the use of pesticides, simply by sending information to the cornfields via a photograph.

The vital signs of an astronaut sent to the moon were monitored even though he was thousands of miles away, and the instrument was not attached to him. The results were identical to NASA's, which were taken via the usual means. A story was published in *Mother-Earth-News*, about a woman in Utah who grew large potato plants with extraordinary success utilizing the support of the SE-5.

Years later we read about an experiment in which a man had used the SE-5 to communicate with dolphins in captivity. The instrument is equipped with a computer, and the researcher connected it to the dolphins' environment by dangling a cable in the water. He typed a question into the computer and asked the dolphins to respond. He found they were eager to communicate. When, with the help of the SE-5, the researcher discovered that one of the dolphins was pregnant, even the trainer was unnerved. "How did you know that? We haven't told anyone!" he declared. The dolphins also communicated their concern about how humans are treating the environment and the negative spiral in which many humans are caught.

This form of technology is obviously not mainstream. It is made possible through the use of dimensions of subtler realities. And dolphins don't need to be convinced of that!

Later Don wrote a book about the wonders of the SE-5 called *Regaining Wholeness Through the Subtle Dimensions*. His interests and abilities have always included some kind of technology. It was also the SE-5 that brought us to the Psychotronic Conference, an exciting annual gathering where many of the scientists who have left the mainstream and are investigating "weird" sciences come together to exchange the latest information, thoughts, and ideas. This conference opens its doors to all scientists and interested lay people and allows them to explore the subtle realms.

About a year before this flight to Hawaii, the time had come for us to lecture at one of the Psychotronic Conferences. Prepared for an adventure, we drove to the conference in Sacramento and were delighted to rub shoulders with others who had found a crack in the door of our normally stable-looking universe. Don and I both shared our excitement over the possibilities of the SE-5 and the impact it had had.

But as much as Don's forte was dealing with technology, mine lay more in the realms of inner realities and psychological processes. I had studied various forms of therapy years before, including breath work, body-centered psychotherapy techniques, Gestalt therapy, Hakomi method, neurolinguistic programming, and so on. None of it, however, had fulfilled my quest for real miracles. For almost six months now I had been asking the universe to guide me toward some method that really, and I meant *really*, could bring about changes. I wanted a key to the giant doorway into the secret dimensions of the universe.

One afternoon at the conference we saw the announcement for a rather promising talk, "Enter the World of the Holographic Universe!"

We sat down in the far upper left side of the auditorium, which had the feeling of an old Grecian amphitheater. The air was full of murmuring and anticipation of yet another great creative mind at play.

5

"Welcome to the holographic universe!" started our speaker. "Don't take anything I tell you as THE TRUTH. Test it for yourself; see if it works; and only then take what you like best and use it in your daily life.

"The universe functions holographically. What you carry in your inner mind reflects itself in the outer world. Please think about that for a moment."

Splash!!! The bright red cherry juice I had been holding in my hands dropped into my lap as I pondered his words. My sparkling white dress was now adorned with a giant, brilliant-red spot. I wondered for a moment about the deeper holographic meaning of this incident. What did I carry in my mind to create such a graphic reflection?

Whatever it was, I needed to wash up. Don could fill me in on the details later.

I quietly slipped out of the auditorium and into the women's bathroom. With the help of soap and water I was able to wash out all the signs of this incident. Outside, the sun beckoned to help dry my dress and provide some long-needed quiet time. I went outside and made myself comfortable on a hilly, grassy spot at the side of the building. Sun rays were soon tickling my face, and I started drifting off, wondering what Don might be learning inside.

Soon I felt my mind lifting out of the present situation. Sensations of flooding light rushed through my body. The air smelled charged with energy and lifted my spirit. I had been laying in this state of appreciation for just a few minutes, when in my mind's eye I found myself listening to a very different kind of speaker. I pretended that I was listening to the lecture, but here we were learning more by doing and feeling rather than by words.

I felt frustrated at being disturbed by the spilling of the juice. Feelings of turmoil were churning in my stomach—I felt disturbed about being disturbed. Caught between these feelings, I suddenly imagined hearing our speaker suggest taking the feelings outside of my body and talking to them. Well, sure, I could do this little exercise. Inwardly I giggled at my creative imagination.

The feeling in my stomach was no less red than the bright juice I had just spilled. I took this irregularly shaped feeling outside myself and let it hover in midair. "Yes, the form of this feeling has just as much sense of Self as you do, and it likes being honored just the same," said my imaginary inner speaker. "Go ahead and ask it what it has been doing for you," he finished.

Reluctantly I sent this question out toward the blob of bright red. "Me? You are really talking to me?" the red blob asked. "Well," the blob continued, "I wanted to make sure you didn't listen to any authority; that's why I got you out of the auditorium."

Oh, I thought. Quite nice of this little fellow, just not what *I* really wanted!

"Go deeper," my speaker's voice said. "Ask this image what it REALLY wants." All right, I did want to know, and so I sent the new question out to the red blob.

It replied, "Well, what I really want is for you to discover the most effective method of transformation, of inner creation and healing from within."

"Wonderful," said my inner mentor. "All you have to ask now is how, if you had already discovered this most miraculous method of transformation, it would look and feel."

Within moments the blob flashed me a feeling-image of what it would look like if I had already found that method. It looked like a bursting fountain of light reflecting many sparkles. The fountain was rising and filling all the space around with a sense of magic. Then it came cascading back down onto itself, now enriched with a plenitude of feeling and knowing, having been touched by many experiences. Then the next wave of cascading sparkles pushed up through the center of the fountain.

That's what being at the center of transformation would look like! I understood that I was looking at the basic matrix of moving in and out of dimensions, of traversing from a black hole to a white hole. If I turned the fountain on its side and looked through the hole in the center, it had the shape of a doughnut. What a miraculous world it could be!

"Now, you are half way there," my inner mentor interrupted my reverie. "You need to honor and thank the old part, the red splash, that wanted to make sure you didn't fall prey to any authority. It really wants something good for you. Sometimes these inner feelings want to throw bombs on everyone and everything so they can create absolute peace. Inside the auditorium you might have missed what I was saying, even though it may have been just what you were looking for. So I'm glad you listened in, and it seems to me, that your new image and feeling of this magical, transformative fountain of light might be able to create the kind of world you're hoping for. Now we need to complete a few more steps, but first you must thank your old image."

OK, I was glad to thank the red splash. After all, I did appreciate its actual intent. I sent the red blob a feeling of gratitude. At least I could thank its deeper, underlying intention to find a magical way of interacting with the creative matrix of the universe.

"Now that your red splash feels your honoring, ask if it is willing to become the new image of the cascading fountain. This *new* image of the doughnut-fountain represents what the red splash wants at its deepest core."

I was surprised to find that the red splash image was all too willing to be part of the new image. Immediately, the red splash floated high up into the air, becoming part of the sparkling light and droplets of the fountain. And then I saw and felt how the red of the splash gave those sparkles a rainbow like hue. Enlivened, the sparkles seemed to glisten even more. A great sense of joy and gratitude flooded me. In all my cells I felt a new surge of energy. "Ask this new image if it is always willing to be there for you, and check to see if you also are always willing to be there for it." When I asked, my new image gave me a resounding "YES!" It was a very comforting feeling of everlasting friendship, and I sent my fountain of light this same welcome and commitment.

"Can you feel the power of commitment?" my inner mentor asked.

I could. And what a feeling it was, so wonderfully assuring and deeply true for me.

"Now, ask your image to go back through all past time and then through all possible futures and heal all events concerned with resisting authority or being the authority yourself. Let it heal all the pain associated with this issue of authority. Let it turn these feelings into the power of accessing your inner wisdom. Let the Miracle of Life be your teacher."

As soon as I sent the request to the cascading fountain to heal my past and future, I could feel my cells starting to buzz. I felt a domino effect pulsing through me and saw brief flashes of struggle reshape themselves into a glorious inner knowing.

What an experience!!! I felt as if I had wings and was swirling in the sunlight with great energy running through my body. "Who are you?" I asked my inner mentor, feeling that I was speaking with someone beyond my own imaginative mind. "I'm a Time Traveler, coming from the future. You have called for your learning to accelerate in order to help humanity, and here I am, one of many who can help point the way. The learning and growing you will have to do yourself."

Exhilarated, I breathed deeply with gratitude. Magical! This world felt magical!

The sun was tickling my nose, and soon I felt the grass beneath my body. My dress had dried, and it was time to go back into the lecture hall. I really had needed the rest. What a great inner journey! I was going to tell Don all about it; I felt I really was onto something.

6

Silently I slipped back into the auditorium. Only twenty-five minutes had passed, and the lecture was still going on. "You won't believe this guy," Don whispered, "you missed a great part of the lecture. He talked about accessing the quantum foam via our imagination. The miracles are for real."

". . . And then the professor transformed the red fireball of anger into what he really wanted," our lecturer said triumphantly, moving his body rhythmically, emphasizing what he was saying. "Remember the fireball he had felt in his stomach?" the lecturer continued. "What this feeling really desired was to be loved, wanted, and accepted. The image of the professor's grandmother had spontaneously appeared in his mind as the perfect holographic image to represent his true desire of being loved.

"He turned the red fireball into an image of his grandmother lovingly passing out cookies to everyone around her.

"As a result of this transformation in his mind, he became the very likable and lovable professor he had really wanted to be. The new images in his mind were not only making him feel good *inside*, they literally created a change in his *outer world*. The next day this same professor had crowds of people hanging around him. Remember, how I told you in the beginning that everything in this universe works holographically? Well, guess what?! Our world *really does* work that way."

Wisdom of the Dolphins

I was dazed. This part of the lecture was almost a rerun of what I had just heard outside in the buzzing warmth of the sun, listening to my inner mind. What was going on? Had the inner mentor not told me he was a Time Traveler and that I had been calling for him? Now it seemed like the lecturer was the source of this information, and I had simply picked it up telepathically. Who was the "real" Time Traveler, the inner one or this lecturer?

Needless to say, Don and I were thrilled by the lecture. During the entire presentation we felt our cells ringing with excitement. From a place deep inside, we *knew* the information presented was true, as though our DNA were singing "Hallelujah!" Looking back on the event, I am glad that our bodily knowledge was so strong. The mind can create endless doubts and questions. How often had I let doubt talk me straight out of a truth? But here I felt in perfect resonance. It was like hearing a bell ring and feeling the same humming in my cells, like waves of harmony overlapping and touching my soul.

We quickly followed the lecturer outside and discovered that he was holding an intensive seminar a few weeks later in the high desert of Arizona. He told us we would be sleeping in yurts and feasting on vegetarian meals in the sun. It would be a time-travel seminar!

I guess I should have known. Maybe this man was real both inside and out. Maybe he was even a real Time Traveler. That would be better than I ever could have dreamed.

7

A few weeks after our first encounter with the Time Traveler, Don and I found ourselves driving to the seminar in the high desert of Arizona. It was early fall, and the air was dry. Indian Summer, with its golden rays of sunlight, caressed our skin.

We arrived mid-afternoon. As we drove up to the Rim Institute, dry pinion trees greeted us, and fallen twigs crackled beneath our feet as we made our way from the parking lot to the registration office. We were to be a small group, mostly couples.

"Ms. Selke, you ordered a vegetarian meal?" asked the flight attendant, pulling me out of my reminiscence about the pungent smells of the pinion forest and back into the present world of jet travel. How deeply I had entered into my daydream reverie! "Yes, I did," I answered, happy to suddenly remember that I was sitting in an airplane on the way to Hawaii. I gently kissed Don's face, grateful beyond words to be able to share so many adventures with him. "I was thinking of our time at the Rim," I told him, wanting to let him know where in the universe I was.

"It is due to what we learned there and what happened afterward that we are taking this trip to see the dolphins," he said. "We learned that our universe functions holographically and how we write the scripts to our life."

With his words still trailing in my ear, I returned to thinking about the food at the Rim Institute and the food we were to have there. One week of gourmet vegetarian food! I looked forward to being nourished inside and out. A dance of balance was needed to live actively in the world, and we needed to nourish our souls with the stillness of the inner dimensions.

In the first few days of our stay at the Institute we were gently led into the rich inner world of our own holographic picture show. We then learned the methods of transformation about which the Time Traveler had lectured weeks earlier at the conference.

With the completion of each exercise, I felt more and more light entering my body. Each of the images I carried inside had at its deepest core a positive intention. No matter how dark a feeling or image was, in the end it wanted to be loved and understood, and then it would let me know what it *really* had wanted to create.

Using the transformation method I never had to decide *for* the problem "image" what would be best for it. I could ask the image for its own wisdom, and it would always tell me or show me what would be best.

It was like slipping into a black hole, and then, when the darkness seemed insurmountable, simply by asking the problem image what it really wanted I was given the new image that would best express the true and deeper need already fulfilled. It felt like bursting through to the white hole that is thought to be on the other side of a black hole. This image transformation is like entering into another dimension by jumping through time and bypassing linear learning. The normal process of learning to express one's highest potential is often accompanied by deep pain. But now I could get to the highest intention of any darkness in a matter of minutes simply by asking.

To be able to bypass linear learning I needed to be willing to consider that goodness is the basis of any evil. "*Evil* is *live* spelled backward," our Time Traveler mentioned in the beginning. "That works great in the English language", I thought. "Yet in German *live* is *leben*, and spelled backward *leben* becomes *Nebel*, which means fog. Even that, however, could be a fitting metaphor for living backward."

Stories abounded of people who had healed their lives by working with our Time Traveler, but this afternoon he told us a story about the time he had wondered whether the changes he made in his own mind had any effect in his world at large.

"And so," our Time Traveler shared on the fourth day of the seminar, "since I could change my inner images and thereby create such dramatic effects in my outer life, I wondered if that would also apply to the larger world." With a pensive voice he continued, "I thought about the poisonous gas in my state, which the government produced and stored in such massive quantities that it could kill the life on planet Earth ninety times over.

"In my inner mind I had an image of what this gas would look like. It was a huge orange cloud. I asked this orange cloud what its purpose was, and it told me that it was maintaining peace by playing war games. It was threatening death in order to maintain peace. So, what it really wanted was to maintain peace."

His voice sounded like he was playing in childlike awe with this gaseous orange cloud. As he built his story, he spoke excitedly, "I asked the image what it would look like if it already had the peace it wanted. With a quick jolt of light it flashed a new image to me, showing how it could maintain peace by playing peace games instead of war games. What a great solution! I finished the process of image transformation, and there I was, walking around with a new image of peace games in the broadcasting station of my mind."

He finished telling us the story. "A few months later I was swimming with dolphins in Florida and met an interesting guy. After we ascertained that we both were active thinkers in the field of quantum physics, I asked him what he did for a living. He told me that until recently he was in charge of war games at the Pentagon. Just recently they had put him in charge of developing peace games!

" Needless to say, my jaw dropped," our Time Traveler concluded thoughtfully. "Was this a mere coincidence, or was there a connection to my inner work?"

At this point in the seminar my own interest was piqued. Shamans from many different cultures are said to summon the powers of nature. They ask for assistance from the rain and cloud beings and work through their visionary powers to restore balance to the community. Could this be a way to access those realms of the shaman's worlds? The image-transformation process we had been learning seemed so simple and very much like only a self-help tool, yet this seminar started to look more like training to become a shaman and a global healer.

/ Ilona Selke

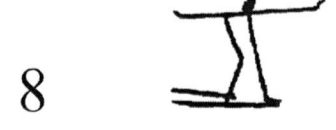

8

The more I became aware of the depth and breadth of this imagery work, the stronger grew my concern about whether we were being tempted by the web of illusion. The implications inherent in the power of this process made me ponder this question deeply.

As taught by many Eastern philosophies, it is best to still the mind and not get caught in the world of appearances. All of manifested life is simply a dance of energy, constantly entertaining the mind. Supposedly this dance is the trap of life; it keeps Soul captivated by its own entertaining show. I needed to find out if this imagery work was headed in the direction of enlightening me or not.

I remember one evening sitting with a woman named Natasha on the rock wall near some pinion trees. The stars were sparkling in the still, warm air. She was a very vibrant woman with exotic features. She looked American Indian and was like a dancing deer with a rich inner world. As we sat there, we started sharing how the new process, however simple, was starting to shake us at our deepest roots. Bit by bit we discovered that we had very similar concerns. What if this was just a temptation pulling us off our spiritual path? I could see how effective this process was by watching each one of us. But hadn't we learned that it is best not to concern ourselves with the world of illusions, best not to try to fix anything in it, since life was a forever-changing mirage? Shouldn't we try to "get out of the lower dimensions" instead of mentally spinning our *tales*?

We decided to ask for inner guidance. We closed our eyes, and with the gentle rhythm of our breath we relaxed and stretched our inner light lines out into the ethers around us. I felt my inner energy field expand. When I imagined a halo of light surrounding me, I began to feel as if I were actually floating.

Slowly, I focused my energy into a star just above my head, as though I were swimming up from the depths of the ocean. Up and up I went until I splashed through the surface of the water. Higher and higher I rose until I could feel myself fully inside the star. Of course, I could still feel the rocks beneath me, but it was more like a background sensation. Now the luminous essence in my star was predominant. Higher and higher I went until I popped out of the sense of being "me" into being just awareness.

Ever higher I went, wanting to ask the "Source-of-All-that-Is" a few questions. I wanted to know if I was just playing with the illusion of life, or if there was a useful purpose behind my new learning. I could sense Natasha's presence as well and felt her shifting in frequencies, becoming a Light without personality.

After a time of moving into an ever-widening sense of being consciousness, I started seeing the ongoing cycle called "Life." Coming and going . . . there was only "Life," for a long . . . long . . . long time . . . for eternity.

I became aware that in this whole process called "Life," God is able to reflect Itself onto Itself. It is experiencing Itself. There was no end in sight. A deep understanding formed in my inner mind. If "Life" in all its formation weren't God's true way of being, then in all the eons of time God could have pulled Its own creation back into Itself, into everlasting Oneness. If dissolution of "Form" and "Creation" indeed would have been the plan, it already would have happened.

Instead I saw all possible worlds of manifestation continuing as an ongoing dance of Life and Consciousness. I felt that God was thrilled by being. In my own life I had noticed that the deepest satisfaction comes from being simultaneously in the still point of knowing God in everything and yet living my current life to the fullest.

I saw how we create reality simply by virtue of what we focus our attention on. It was as if I, as a human, was learning to become a conscious dreamer in the Great Dream of the One, allowing God to see Itself, reflecting Itself through my eyes.

I was learning to love the darkness and understand that everything has a radiant potential hidden within it. I didn't need to fight, ignore, or even vaporize the darkness. All I had to do was open my heart and know that deep inside, everything has a positive intention; everything is made of the same substance called Life, originating in God.

As a result I was free to let the darkness in me become the light. Deeper yet, I learned to realize that all Darkness is Light in disguise, and all Light is Darkness from a higher perspective. It is all part and parcel of the checker board game called "Reality", the quantum foam.

Slowly, I let go of my doubts, starting to feel my inner dimensions take on more and more understanding. Life is perhaps more about being aware and expressing the inherent God energy in everything than it is about getting out of the "mess" called Life.

Perhaps ecstasy is the result of knowing the Source, being one with it, while expressing the Source in all possible ways. Oneness *and* diversity at the same time were the answer, not one *or* the other.

Finally I felt satisfied. I sent the information back through space and time in order to start anchoring it in my human mind. This portion is vital to all my inner journeying, as I need to record the information in my mental body. As I sent the information back to my human self, it was as if I could see the light of the information filtering through the dimensions, cascading through the inner worlds, arching back like a fountain of water until it touched the bottom of its own pool, pulling it through the earth and my own body, now ready to be assimilated. This way I could record the information and recall what I had learned.

Slowly I started feeling myself surrounded by the pinion trees again, thankful to be living in a vibrant sea of consciousness in action. I sent gratitude to All-that-Is and assembled myself in the physical dimension with clarity.

Natasha had come back about the same time. "Did you get an answer?" we asked almost simultaneously. "What a journey I had," she mused. "It seemed like we both were traveling along similar roads."

Satisfied, we thought of the coming day. We would dive into the world of Time Travel.

"I wonder what Time Travel will be like, especially if we can see real changes?" I mused. We walked a while in silence, feeling the trees touching our skin, touching our souls, and whispering their good-night to us.

9

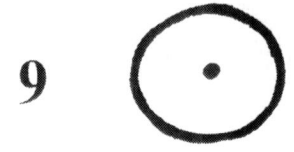

The next day our Time Traveler was going to show us how incredibly interconnected life, time, and the imagination really are. Objective Time Travel would lose its appeal, he told us, as we would traverse the imaginary boundary of internal and external time.

I still remember the first lecture he gave us. "Time and space have different properties in different dimensions," he stated matter of factly. "We humans, here in the three-dimensional world, experience time mostly linearly. What I do now has its consequences tomorrow.

"Time seems to have something to do with expressing potentials and with learning. One choice after another can be experienced, and the consequences can be observed. If you think about it, if life is like a school where one can observe the effects of one's actions and learn from them, or simply enjoy watching one's creation unfold, then time as we know it has great value.

"The experience of undergoing the process of aging, for example, is fascinating. The shift in hormones throughout one's lifetime brings about different thought processes and different ways of relating to other people. Grandmothers wouldn't be the same if they had the same hormones floating through their bodies as they did when they were teenagers. They would be looking for the right mating partner instead of cuddling grandbabies.

"The sequence of time is really very endearing. Love

becomes meaningful, since it can be experienced, observed, and felt in action. The joy of uniting one's body or soul with another can only happen because there is a separateness or sequential nature to manifestation.

"You may be wondering why I am exalting the experience of being *in* time. If you recall how we dealt with transforming so-called 'negative patterns' earlier, you will remember that we always looked to see how they had served us, what they had given us, and then we appreciated them for what they really wanted.

"To be free of any bondage is to be able to appreciate the limitation for what it has provided us. What is the hidden gift? If we feel trapped by time and can't appreciate its gift to us, we can never be free of its hold on us.

"So let's look at how our human lineage has gifted us. What are the gifts of your family tree?" our Time Traveler asked. "Somehow all your ancestors have woven a brilliant thread through your family's lives. Choices upon choices, hidden or not—all brought a gift of which you are now the ultimate bearer. What do these gifts mean to you? Look behind the obvious negativity they seem to hold," he finished.

I mused over my gifts. Creativity, awe of nature, multicultural abilities, intuition, love of travel, love of simple things, multiple languages, genetic disposition—good or bad—access to invisible worlds. But there were also the painful events, the sorrow and loss. After we looked at these issues more deeply, it appeared that challenges were also potential gifts.

My father's death when I was two years old made me

search through the inner dimensions to feel his presence, and it opened me to the subtle worlds. Painful as the experience of his loss had been, a gift was hidden within it. I learned to be sensitive to other levels and dimensions of life.

It wasn't always easy for all of us in the group to see the hidden gifts, especially when abuse was part of the picture, but we saw the riches of time gifting an unlimited array of possibilities for expression and learning.

"Soon we will each be traveling into an aspect of the past that holds a very important key for us. When we are able to sense the deeper pattern in seemingly chaotic lives, we will be able to recognize how life is designed to provide an opportunity for Love to express itself. You will be able to see beyond the confines of abuse, war, fighting, etc. All of these threats are silent calls for Love, the hidden face of God shining through everything.

"During these last few days we have been building a field of resonance. The images that you have been working with are sacred beings. They are helping you and are as real as any other being you know. The red rose of love, the pyramid, the big oak—all are symbolic images for your mind. In reality, the way I can explain it, these images are more like Spirit helpers from a much deeper reality.

"The energy of Love now has a way of becoming part of your life. The red rose is now like your new song on your inner radio station. Whereas before you might have been playing songs of sorrow and pain over and over, now you are sending out a new resonant field, a song of Love. The old energy has gone through a maturation process. You have learned from it, understood that time and linear learning are not the only ways to operate, and you have jumped through time into a new dimension.

"By retaining the transformed image, one that now expresses what you/it really wanted to have, you can create a new reality. You dream your world anew. If you are willing to see beauty around you, experience the purpose for learning in any given circumstance, and realize your part in co-creating the dream of Life, you are ready to navigate through time.

"Imagine that you have been given a doorway from your three-dimensional universe to your multidimensional universe. You build the field; the rest will come."

He paused for a while, sitting in silence, looking out onto the distant shores of time. The web of crossing lines, made up of light, was expanding itself in front of his vision. He knew the time was coming quickly for some members of our group to start on their journey through time. Perhaps even this afternoon.

10

Lunch had been exceptionally good, vegetarian gourmet food in the middle of a high-altitude desert! Slowly Don and I strolled through the forest paths, enjoying a few minutes to ourselves. He looked at me with such luminous eyes, beaming with love and joy. Often times his eyes reminded me of an eagle or an angel.

I opened the door to the yurt where the seminar took place and it made a muffled squeak. The sunlight was beaming golden rays into this tent-like dwelling. It reminded me of American Indian times. As soon as we entered we noticed our Time Traveler hunched off to the side intently listening to Natasha, who was laying on the floor. She was weeping. We quickly got filled in. Natasha had felt the field of the time web becoming pregnant and had declared herself ready. She didn't go to lunch, but sat waiting, letting the field lift her spirit.

Now she was seeing the "Trail of Tears" in her inner journey back through time. At first she witnessed the vision from far above, her soul wrenched by the pain endured by the American Indians on the trail. But then one of her inner travel guides volunteered to assist her on her journey. He advised her from the perspective of her Highest Self, showing her that she needed to look into the pain of the past. If she didn't, the withdrawal would keep her in a frozen state of incomprehension, which had been affecting her life in many ways. But now she could unfold the power and realize the depth of compassion and learning that would result from her journey into the past.

She now had the maturity required for this journey. What followed at first were gruesome feelings, scenes of fighting and blood flowing, of hatred or resignation between the white people and the American Indians.

No one in our group remained untouched. We could all feel the events of time, each in our own way.

I felt like I might well have been one of the American Indians myself. The irony of it was that I was now a white person, although from Germany, living on land that had previously been the home of the American Indians. The sorrow I felt in my heart for these people was deep. How much pride had we/they felt in taking care of the spirit of the land! Why did this happen; what had gone wrong? I was equally immersed in the events, seeing before my eyes the scenes of the decimation of the Indian Nation.

Natasha's inner guide took her to the Place of Planning, where all beings were present in their luminous glow. She saw the light surrounding each and every one of the players in the Trail of Tears drama. Here at the Place of Planing all the beings communed in a deep way. The lesson they were about to learn was a lesson of love, of forgiveness, of seeing the interchangeable nature of each of the players. Blood was shed, but it could have been a communion. What really was wanted was for each one to realize that the lesson was about transcending the sense of separation. It was a difficult lesson, and many beings incarnated over and over again in many different situations to learn this profound lesson. Natasha had been an American Indian, then a settler, and could now see how each one wanted to continue his or her own survival and tradition.

She had been Soul, experiencing the difficulties from all sides. In truth, she was neither an "American Indian" nor a "settler" in her Soul. Beyond the choices of learning Love and the inherent Oneness of all life, in her Soul she was free.

Yet still she struggled with this learning. This lifetime she had been a "white" person, looking much like an American Indian. Her pain of living on the land as a white person had bothered her deeply. Now she was beginning to see the beauty of all beings traveling on the Trail of Learning.

Our Time Traveler asked if her inner guide could give her an image of the depth of learning, of the understanding of Soul living in so many different guises, all of which serve learning the lesson of Love and Oneness. A brilliant rosette-shaped crystal showed itself to her. Filled with the deep knowing of the Love inside the enemy's heart, the rosette was asked to go into all the scenes of past sorrow and suffering and heal all those events. Deep understanding of Oneness permeated her cellular knowledge of past, present, and future.

As ripples ran through her body, shivers of learning settled into her cellular being. Her inner body-mind would not be able to tell the difference between imagined and "real" experiences. To her internal system it would be the same.

According to our Time Traveler she not only was healing her own inner being, transforming old emotions and memories, but also contributing to the healing of all those on the Trail of Tears in the inner web of time. Not until later would I see how much bigger than our personal life this imagery work would be. Inner and outer would blend and become interchangeable.

Natasha was letting the deep understanding of Love and Oneness settle into her. Then her inner guide took her to a futuristic place, where we all got a glimpse of a new way of incarnating. Instead of assuming only one life form, we could now roll in and out for much shorter periods of time. When the task as one form was completed, we could simply roll out of that body and move on to a different one. One moment we might be a tiger, the next an extraterrestrial. Some other suitable soul that wished to have the experience we just left behind could take over the body we had just slipped out of.

In some ways, this ability was congruent with what we had previously learned on the Trail of Tears. The essence of learning is being able to slip in and out of forms to gain experience without overly identifying with any one of them. It was fun to ride along on this journey. New job descriptions could come into the marketplace, such as "Inner Guide to Multidimensional Tours."

Next it was my turn.

11

I created a little cove for myself with pillows and blankets and prepared for my journey. It was to be unlike any of the previous imagery exercises. Not until I had laid down and invited my spirit guide to take me on the journey back to a time that held a knot for me did I realize that the "field" about which our Time Traveler had spoken was truly a place of entry into another dimension. As though I were being lifted by energized hands, I began floating and going into fast-moving scenes of images.

Suddenly the shifting of images stopped and I found myself in a large stone building. I recognized the sculpting of the stones as Aztec architecture. At first I saw gruesome images of torture and cages, too frightening to look at. But as my guide took me along, we looked at the lesson that this lifetime still held frozen for me.

I had been a priest, and despite knowing that the doctrines of worship were false and the sacrifices useless, I had kept quiet. I had not spoken the truth, believing that I would be killed if I did. That could well have been the case, but the burden I still carried from that time was a sense of unfulfilled responsibility. I had judged the people who simply followed, behaving like sheep, and by distancing myself I had created an excuse for my behavior, a way out.

What I really had wanted was to express the truth in an egoless way, shining the light of the spirit worlds, and to show how we all can be in touch with God, which we are at the core of our essence. The image that now came to me was a luminous being standing with outstretched arms, clad in a white garment, radiating brilliance. I let this image begin to transform my old fears and judgments, now becoming the radiance of Truth, Love, and Spirit.

It felt like I had let go of a very old iceberg weighing on my soul. My judgment of others and myself lifted and transformed into compassion, understanding, and the desire to share from my heart. I began to feel the change ripple through my body. Waves of aliveness and joy pulsed through me. I felt like the portal of time was opening and letting me rewrite the scripts of old pains to reflect the beauty that had always been there awaiting me.

As I felt this ripple of change come to completion, I asked inwardly whether the full transformation was complete. My inner guide quickly brought me to yet another experience, although much more recent in time.

I was taken back in this lifetime, to age three. I had been born in Kabul, Afghanistan, and spoke Persian as well as German during my first few years. As an early talker I had soon been fluent in both languages.

In this scene I found myself trying to speak to my mother, but she said over and over that she couldn't understand me. No matter how many times I repeated myself, she didn't get it. I became extremely frustrated. From then on I assumed that figuratively I must be speaking Greek, and that I could not effectively communicate with people. In front of groups of people I felt even worse. Were my concepts so out of this world? Or had I so little command over the choice of words and syntax? I believed the latter had to be true.

Now I was reviewing my experience. My father had died while we were living in Afghanistan. Due to Afghan law no foreign woman was allowed to live there without a husband, and thus my mother had to prepare us to return to Germany.

I had been speaking Persian and German, and everyone had always understood me. Now, my mother was trying to get me used to speaking only German, and eventually she refused to understand me when I spoke Persian. I did not understand her intent, however, and she had no idea how engraved that experience would become on my subconscious mind.

Now, with insight and inner guidance, I asked for resolution. This blockage of language had been connected to the experience of not speaking the truth in Aztecan times and was carried over into this lifetime. I felt that no matter how much I tried, I couldn't get my point across. It was as though I were speaking a foreign language. With the wisdom of the inner worlds, my inner mind presented me with the solution: a rainbow of multilayered colors was to become my translation beam. From now on it would automatically translate all my words into easily understandable words, expressions, and concepts.

I could feel the ripple of change arching back into the far distant past, traveling through my childhood and reaching into my future. It was as though my inner cells were undergoing a restructuring. A deep sense of well-being flooded through me, creating an inner sense of harmony that stretched far beyond the boundaries of the "me" in this world.

Perhaps my changes "in here" created changes "out there." Maybe "out there" was in many ways a reflection of my inner dreaming. If that was true, then we all are much more connected and powerful in creating positive changes than we usually assume. Years later I found out how true this is and how closely it is related to the indigenous way of thinking.

My journey had come to a natural completion, and my guide took me back through the dimensions and layers of the inner worlds. All my learning assembled into a meaningful whole, and I started sensing the love of the group around me. Like a clan, everyone had gathered around and was welcoming me back to this world with a birthday song. A new birth! A deeper part of me coming forward!

As I sat up and started speaking, a woman in the group gazed at me in awe. She had previously had trouble understanding what I had been saying, but now she said she could understand me with ease.

Whether it was the "field" in the moment that prompted her to say this I do not know, but shortly thereafter I found myself in front of audiences of several hundred people, giving lectures and being complimented on my ability to translate such complex issues into layman's terms. These changes withstood the test of reality, and I was glad.

12

As I was shifting in my airplane seat, I noticed the appealing smells of food drifting down the aisles. All my imagery learning had brought me here on this journey to find dolphins in the wild. I had applied specific imagery steps to create the possibility of being here on this flight. Dolphins had started coming to me in my dreams and had begun to show me how the world of inner dreaming was affecting outer realities.

It had started at Sea World in California, just after we first met the Time Traveler.

Don and I had bought tickets to Sea World on a hot afternoon. We had arrived just in time to see the orca whale show. Orcas are the largest of the dolphins and have been misleadingly called killer whales. The big black and white spots of the orca we saw, were making this beautiful being look like a toy. As he swam into the "big" performance pool my eyes flooded with tears and my heart started pounding. How could anyone with any brains at all ask a being like this to perform "tricks"? Imagine the reverse situation being imposed on humans? The whales probably wouldn't have it in them to do that sort of thing.

Feelings were engulfing me from an unknown source. I had never thought much about whales or dolphins before. But I *knew* that this orca could feel far beyond what many humans could. The immensity of this being's presence spoke to me from a far deeper level than I could rationalize. Partially it felt like this orca was sending telepathic communications. Although I could not make out specific thoughts, I knew that I was receiving something beyond the scope of my understanding. Later I learned that many people experience an overwhelming heart opening feeling when they see dolphins or whales. In their presence, people often feel inexplicable joy, at times even bordering on ecstasy.

I made a resolution after the show: I was never going to give my direct or indirect support to keeping whales or dolphins captive. That was the least I could do.

Our visit to Sea World shook up both Don and me. We got into heated arguments and decided not to eat tuna anymore. At that time many dolphins were being killed by drowning in fishing nets used to catch tuna.

Evolution has given these sea mammals bigger brains and more complex neocortexes than humans. The degree to which the neocortex is folded into crevices has been shown to be indicative of the intelligence of a given species. Until only recently it was assumed that humans had the most complex brain structure. That changed, however, when scientists found that bottlenose dolphins, like Flipper, have more complex and dense gray matter than humans do. Or even when the cortex was less dense, the number of connections between neurons has been shown to be equal to humans in complexity. Now came the big question: Where did this surprising discovery place humans in the hierarchy of intelligence?

Since our mammalian cousins have not created anything of lasting value, it is assumed that they cannot be as intelligent as, and certainly not more intelligent than, humans.

But what if building structures, like ants do, is not necessarily a sign of superiority? What if inner wisdom, the ability to love, being able to evolve in consciousness, and refraining from destroying the planet are of more value? As all these thoughts flooded through me, I started wondering where they were coming from.

My attention was riveted! A deep compassion for these sea mammals filled my heart, and as a result I soon joined Greenpeace.

One night, a few months after the seminar at the Rim Institute, I had a dream: Three dolphins were in a big tank. The water had partially leaked out and the dolphins were threatened by the possibility of suffocation. I didn't realize in my dream that the lack of water did not necessarily mean suffocation to dolphins, but oh well, such are dreams. Somehow I created a stir in my dream and got the attention of others to help these suffocating dolphins. After considerable effort we were able to save two of them; the third one died during our attempted rescue.

Unknown to me, at the time I had my dream, there had been news about three whales in Alaskan waters who had been trapped by an ice shelf and could not swim back into the open sea. The air holes in the ice through which they were able to breathe were getting smaller and smaller, threatening to suffocate them.

At the time, as is true today, I didn't watch television or read the newspaper. For my taste, too much brain washing and waste of energy was due to the media . But a few days after I had my dream I walked past a newspaper stand, and the headlines almost jumped out at me: "Two Whales

Saved." The third one had died! I knelt down and read the story. Was I dreaming? It was so reminiscent of my dolphin dream that I really began to wonder. Did the whales send out a message? Did my dream solution help in some way? Had my dream helped create a change in physical reality? And why did I dream of dolphins instead of whales? Maybe dolphins were easier to understand mentally and their thought structure easier for humans to follow. Maybe the dolphins were better messengers, at least for me. Of course it could simply be that in dreams we interpret images according to what we can most easily conceive.

One thing was for sure: Dreaming was not solely a reflection of my own subconscious longing or unfulfilled desires, as Freud might have thought. My dream somehow reflected and interacted with the real world "out there," even if I had only telepathically connected with people's attention on this event, without consciously knowing about it.

The coincidence of the solution of the whale's problem "in the real world" with my dream rescue made me wonder. It marked the beginning of my being called by the dolphins.

13

"Ham or beef? Would you like ham or beef, madam?" asked a voice repetitiously. "Ahh, neither, thanks," I said, as I was startled out of my reverie. I quickly remembered where I was. "We ordered vegetarian meals," I added smiling. Don had fallen asleep next to me, and we were both being roused by the food service. The flight attendant checked the kitchen and brought us two delicious veggie meals. Hawaii was coming closer.

As I peeked through my half-closed eyes, I pondered the difference between dreams, visions, and our future. This solid world started looking more and more flexible. Ideas were turning more quickly into realities. If my grandfather had had a vision, when he was young, of traveling in a flying machine, he might have thought this vision could only come true in thousands of years in the future. Instead, airplanes were invented just a few years after his childhood in Germany, where he traveled by horse and buggy, at most a few miles away from home.

Here I was in my early thirties jetting from one country to the next in planes that didn't even exist in plans when my grandfather was young. Telephones, electric stoves, even washing machines—are all very recent developments. Satellites zoom around the earth beaming endless strings of information and images worldwide in an instant.

Someone always has a dream, a vision, before discovering the way to get there. The people who transform ideas into reality often have a vision and a sense of mission and acknowledge their imagination as the tool that brings everything to pass.

We are all navigating together as a collective consciousness. Some people have big dreams and great visions which become an inspiration to others, fueling them to manifest these dreams.

Has it not been the dreams of strong individuals, of visionaries, of writers that have inspired the imagination of many, laying the groundwork for future creations? Did not the hopes and wishes of young dreamers turn into the inspiration and drive that led to discoveries when they became adults? How much has Jules Vernes, with his futuristic tales, influenced our thinking? Are we all somehow wishing and dreaming our experiences into being, collectively and individually? Surely it is our imagination that spurs us on and helps us choose a particular path.

I remember playing as a child with my sister. We had the habit of setting our dolls at the end of our beds and then pretending we were them while making up imaginary adventures. We, of course, had supernatural powers. Our imaginations were strong enough to change events. We could speak different languages fluently; we could fly; and we were detectives for the Good.

One time we flew over a forest. In a clearing below us we saw a lake surrounded by a meadow. What puzzles me to this day is the fact that we could see each other's scenes as though they were our own. We didn't have to tell each other anything; we literally both saw the same things. Did we travel to the same inner dimensions?

This particular day in our imagination we descended to the lake. As soon as we landed in the soft grass, however, we sensed danger. An ominous presence was permeating the pristine air. The sight of a big van nearby with some rough characters sitting in it signaled us to become invisible and listen in. They were stealing the hair of the miniature mermaids who lived in the lake, and then sold it for a fortune in the cities.

We instantly dived into the water and looked at the situation for ourselves. Sure enough, the mermaids were in shock. They were in deep despair and had called out for our help. We, of course, used our magical abilities and freed the mermaids from their plight. The bad guys had to face justice, never quite figuring out how those fairy mermaids and two little girls could bring them to their knees.

When I became an adult, I felt like part of my childhood fantasies were starting to come alive. The mermaids had turned into dolphins, and in time I would help them as much as I could.

If we do lay the seed for many of our accomplishments in our childhood dreams, as well as in our daydreams, then the world is in big need of help now. Many children, as well as adults, spend their time absorbing other people's dreams via television, advertisements, and many negative movies. Under the guise of needing to be informed, television is sold to the public as a way of being in touch. Yet, in actuality, television is perhaps the biggest factor in families *not* being in touch. Staring straight ahead in the same direction, isolated in their own emotional world, the true closeness and togetherness does not happen easily for television watchers. Television's substitute dreams seem to be running the show. What if these dreams come true, like they have a habit of doing?

If it became a sign of intelligence, creativity, and self-awareness to throw out one's television—and not just hide behind the line: "I only watch National Geographic programs"—I believe more people would start dreaming their own dreams by realizing they are in the driver's seat of their lives.

The attraction our mind has to images is powerful—both inner or outer images. At the same time, this desire is a great tool and makes us dream, daydream, wish and hope, and expand beyond the limits of the three-dimensional world. It helps us move onward in our quest to find the Source of Life.

Once we give our mind the easy way out, however, by supplying it with moving pictures from the outside, addiction sets in. And because watching television is socially accepted, and one is so belittled if one doesn't "stay in touch," nobody threatens to end this hypnotic addiction.

It's almost like a global amnesia.

I remember a conversation with a woman who had recently lost her son. She told me about a transcendental experience she had with him for a brief period after his death. He stayed in close touch for a few weeks and communicated with her. Every message, direction or instruction he gave, was miraculously confirmed. Then one day she asked him to answer a question: "What is the single most destructive thing mankind is doing that by changing it would be of greatest benefit?"

The answer was spelled out clearly: "Get rid of the TV!"

This shocked her, as it was certainly not an answer she expected. Of course, she got rid of her television immediately. The message from her son had been that strong.

14

"Remember the Rim Institute, Don, when we went backward through imaginary events in time, recreating our past in order to help initiate healing of leftover blockages?" I asked, after we had finished eating. "How do we know that it has anything at all to do with the past, with Time Traveling, and is not just a nice internal movie? How do we know that we are actually dealing with the element of time?"

Thoughtful as always, he took his time answering. His blue eyes wandered over the cloudscape outside the window, searching in faraway lands. I sensed him moving his inner perception to ever-higher inner planes. We all navigate through these inner worlds quite often, but we consider it so absolutely normal that we don't often give it much credit. Don knew the answers were all available inside, if we could but grasp their meaning.

"We seem to separate time as though it is a linear event," he said, as if talking from another world. "But time is much more like a fabric, like the dream fabric. If we re-dream any part of the memory fabric, then it creates ripples through the entire surrounding fabric as well. Remember the guy at one of the seminars who had never heard his father say anything nice, had not even been given a toy by him? When he underwent the imagery healing of his past, he saw that he and his father really had wanted to learn to love one another. He could understand the pain and blockages they both had lived through, and then he let Love heal his past. When he returned home from the week-long seminar, he had a message on his answering machine from his dad. For the first time in his life, his dad told him that he loved him," Don reminisced.

I remembered that the same thing had happened to a couple of people after subsequent seminars we attended.

"The father was changed," Don continued. "He changed without having been told anything, without any outward communication that could have triggered such a drastic transformation. Since the only change that had been made was in the dream fabric, it seems clear that we are able to re-dream the past, thereby creating changes in the here and now and also creating a different future."

Was the true Time Machine **within us**? Was it our consciousness and focus that shifted and shaped the dream fabric of life? As dreamers we illuminate consciously or unconsciously the many possibilities of the One, of God in action.

"You know," Don said after a while, "we've experienced some pretty dramatic time-shifting events, which were so puzzling that they put to rest all our questions about the reality of the imagination. Remember our trip to Stuttgart?" I certainly did!

One year after the first seminar at the Rim Institute, Don and I went to Germany to teach a seminar, as well as to visit friends and family. One day we took the train south to see a close friend of mine. We had arranged to meet him at the train-station, in Stuttgart, having given him our time of arrival and gate number. Unfortunately, we made our arrangements shortly before he moved to a new apartment, and so we did not have his new address or phone number.

Right from the start of our trip everything seemed to move slowly, like molasses. The train was delayed and had to stop every so often due to work on the rails. We passed one train station after another, all displaying the traditional clocks. Time had not slowed down—although it felt like it—and it did not look like we would catch up, being forty-five minutes late already. As I sat in the small compartment, I started getting aggravated. Anger and frustration built up inside me. There was little I could do other than sit and wait. I was especially upset because I knew our friend, being a classical musician, still had a rehearsal that afternoon, and I had no way of getting a message to him, nor could I find out where he had moved to. We had really put ourselves into a corner, but German trains are supposedly always on time, and we really hadn't expected to be delayed.

My frustration and anger started clouding my mind and heart, and I found myself talking to myself. The least I could do was use the imagery process we had learned from our Time Traveler. We had been using it for almost every instance in life that needed problem-solving. At first I sneered at the thought, but then I gave in.

My image answered truthfully, "What I really want is to be there on time."

I sighed and thought, "All I'll be able to do is make myself feel better. But at least I will not be steaming mad."

As I transformed my anger into its true desire, which was, *to be greeted by our friend on time,* I laughed silently. What a joke! Here I was, imagining being on time, whereas all the clocks along the way kept reminding me of the futility of my little wish. At the end of the session I did feel better, however. At least I was able to see the resolution in my inner mind and feel more peaceful.

Finally we reached Stuttgart. We had not been able to speed up time and therefore arrived at a different gate, the original already being occupied. We dragged our luggage to the head of the platform, and Don decided to walk around while I stayed with our bags. Maybe our friend was waiting for us somewhere. Suddenly Don and Ali came skipping down the platform. "What are you doing here so early?" Ali asked, giggling. I took a quick look at the oversized railway clock and almost gasped. He wasn't kidding. We were early!

But how could that be? It takes several hours to get to Stuttgart; there aren't any time-zone changes in Germany; and we had experienced long delays. We watched the clocks all the way to Stuttgart, and we were going to be late due to all the rail work. And we were late—at least until we actually arrived in Stuttgart. It was such a puzzle that we could never find a rational explanation for this shift in time. Only the internal work I had done seemed to give some kind of clue.

A very similar event had happened on a trip to Taos, New Mexico. A dear friend of ours from Boulder, Colorado, happened to be passing through Taos while we were visiting a researcher in Santa Fe. We arranged with our friend, Mark, by phone to meet at a specific time near one of the gas stations in Taos.

This time we were delayed by a late start. While Don

and I were giving a lecture at a conference in Denver, we met a fascinating scientist and researcher with whom we were now visiting in Santa Fe. Our discussions and philosophizing during breakfast made us forget the time and we got a late start as a result.

Sitting in the passenger seat, again I sensed the pressure of wanting and needing to meet with our friend Mark on time. Knowing that it took about one hour to get to Taos I was very concerned when I realized that our scheduled meeting time was in thirty minutes. Would our friend wait for us? We didn't even know the exact location of the gas station where we were supposed to meet.

My anxiousness nauseated me. The least I could do was address my feelings by getting in touch with my body and the internal imagery with which I was so familiar by now. I went through the process of accessing the feeling in my body, finding out what it really wanted, and then letting it give me the image of that wish fulfilled. Irrational as it seemed, this feeling simply wanted to be on time and meet our friend. The fulfilled image looked like a rainbow over the desert. Immediately I started to feel better and my energy had returned by the end of the imagery process.

On the way we saw a sign stating that we had thirty miles to go, and yet I realized that we had only five minutes remaining. We needed at least another half hour! As we pulled into Taos I checked our clock. What? We were here on time?! Impossible! Mark suddenly appeared in his car, driving into town from the other direction. The town had only one main road, and we spotted each other at the same time.

Had it not been for our energetic hello, so filled with the joy of seeing each other, I probably would have found myself on the floor in a state of disbelief. Was this real? Did I make a mistake looking at the clock? Had the sign stating we had thirty miles to go been in the wrong place? What on earth was going on?

This meant that we were creating anomalies in time and space by the use of our imagination. Life *is* as we dream it. This was becoming more and more clear to us.

15

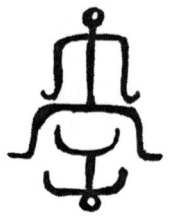

While we were talking about time and our experiences, I had been gently touching Don's leg as he sat next to me in the plane. My eyes met his, and I could feel us both open our inner awareness to one another. It was as though not only our bodies touched, but we also reached into our souls, touching and dancing with each other there. Smiling, I rolled my head onto his shoulder and kissed his neck.

Our hands found each other, and with them we engaged the dance of loving excitement. He took the lead and seduced my fingers so sensuously, coming in closer, then teasingly pulling away, awakening in me more and more desire. Then I took the cue, and following along in my inner vision as though I could see how our souls were touching and intertwining ever more deeply, I guided our hands into a climbing rhythm and increasingly sensuous oneness, slipping along and over his fingers with mine, alluding to other kinds of dancing together. We were breathing in harmony and held our heads closely together. Our breath told us more about how we felt than any words ever could.

The subtle changes in our sighs and breaths merged with our auric fields of color flowing in and out of each other with increasing speed. We were bathing in a joyous circle. Lovemaking has so many dimensions. Sometimes we just sit across from one another and follow the flow of ecstasy inwardly without ever moving the body.

Unlike dolphins, however, I felt shy about people looking in on us, at least in real life. Dolphins do not have walls to hide behind; they share sensuality in plain view of everyone. What sets dolphins apart from other animals is that they seem to have sexual exchanges for the sole purpose of enjoyment, much like humans, and do not only mate when in "heat."

As Don and I came to a natural resting point in our dance, we caressed each other's hands and faces. Our hearts and bodies were glowing.

Soon we would be landing in Hawaii, allowing our dream to unfold. My mind turned to the weeks to come. We would be camping, exposed to the elements. Kauai is known as the garden island, being lush, tropical, and full of natural beauty. We had no idea where and when we would meet dolphins, but that was our primary interest.

The book I had been reading talked about water births and how in some cases dolphins have assisted such events. One Russian doctor by the name of Igor Tcharkovsky has worked with women giving birth in the Black Sea, where dolphins have been present at the time of delivery. The children return every year to the Black Sea, as do "their" dolphins, sharing in an intuitive bond that seems to nourish both dolphins and humans.

The long-term effects seem to be that the children have stronger immune systems, are able to swim underwater for up to eight minutes, have stronger intuitive abilities, and are less irritable and generally happier.

The idea of a weightless birth in water makes so much sense! Imagine flowing from warm body fluids out into warm water and then slowly being lifted onto the chest of your mother's warm, sensuous, naked body lying in the water. She greets you softly with her touches. What a beginning!!!

I was so excited to read about this just as we went on our trip. In my mind I imagined how Don and I would make love in the ocean with dolphins all around.

I was ready to meet dolphins! I had little idea of how much I had to evolve before I would come "face to face" with them! There was no guide, no navigator, to introduce us to one another. And first of all, we had to find them.

"Ladies and gentlemen," the announcement pulled me out of my reverie, "we are approaching Honolulu airport and will be landing in twenty minutes." The captain went on to describe some of the land features below us and thanked us for flying with them. We had shifted into another universe at the beginning of our flight, or perhaps we had re-dreamed the fabric of reality in which we moved. We were glad that we didn't have to spend a night in Honolulu.

Everything is intertwined in life. Imagery is a major key in creating the kind of life we want to live. Many times it is our unconsciously held beliefs that limit the life we can have. The miracles are always in balance and in harmony with our innermost belief systems.

After only a brief stop we were on our last flight, a short island hop to Kauai. Don looked out the window of our little propeller airplane and enjoyed the landscape below us. There was beautiful turquoise water, and as Kauai came into view we found ourselves marveling at a mountain shrouded in clouds in the middle of the island. Massive greenery lay elsewhere beneath a few scattered clouds.

After we landed, Hawaiian music started to float through the air. "Aloha and welcome to Hawaii and mahalo for flying with us today on this journey to paradise," said a flight attendant over the loudspeaker. We were excited.

16

We stepped out of the airplane into warm, balmy air. It was late afternoon and the sun would be setting soon. Palm trees were swaying in a light breeze, thrilling my senses. It was our first time to set foot on this island. Situated in the middle of the ocean, I could feel that a different rhythm pulsed through the lives of the people here.

Where were we going to sleep tonight; where were we going to turn; who were we going to meet? Our trip started to feel like an adventure. We knew only one thing for sure: We would try to find dolphins!

The first night was so unpleasant, however, that I wanted to go home. As we lay in our tent falling asleep, the wind picked up and started to flatten the tent on top of us. When it finally touched our noses and the rain came down—a regular occurrence on Kauai—we headed for the car and fitfully slept in the seats. We forgot our midnight pledge to go home when the morning light woke us with the smell of tropical air and the exotic sound of the birds.

It took us about one week to get our bearings, to find out which hikes were good, where the natural food stores were, and in which bay we could find the most colorful fish. We got used to the ocean, and I practiced snorkeling in shallow water. Don had never snorkeled before, and just putting his head underwater was an exciting event. At Poipu Beach we discovered the joy of weightlessness as we lazed around in the water looking at fish. We let go of all attempts at holding ourselves "up." Letting our hands and legs dangle freely, totally unrestrained, we just floated, marveling at the light patterns of the sun being reflected on the sand.

We hung motionless in the water, very similar to floating in a flotation tank. Since I didn't need to pay attention to my body and no gravity was pulling on me, I was free to be mesmerized by the light patterns as my body was caressed by the lulling waves. Here in the shallow part of the water I felt safe enough, and everything else faded away. I let go of all thoughts, bodily distractions, emotions, and worries, and only the waves of light caught my attention. A deep sense of well-being filled my body, and I started making friends with the ocean.

Water hadn't been my natural "'home," and it always took a bit of coaxing to get me into it. This was probably not the best feeling to have if I were going to meet dolphins, since they are always in the water. I didn't know it at the time, but before I could be with dolphins I needed to work on a number of fears in myself and deal with deep-seated anxieties. One of these was a fear of deep ocean water.

"Dear ones," I sent a message to the dolphins in the underwater world, "I come in Love and with the desire to be with you. Would you please come and meet with me?"

I was sure the water would carry my intent to them. In my mind I imagined the dolphins somewhere out there receiving my message, and me here in the water sending my plea. Little did I know that I was maintaining the distance between us by continuously imagining it.

We had come to Kauai to discover the magic of dolphins,

but as yet had encountered none. We heard that boats were often greeted by dolphins playing in the bow wave, but we wanted to *swim with them*, or at least *near* them, so we didn't take any boat tours.

Then one day we met some very kind island people who told us about a magical cave near the ocean where we could camp at night, but they told us we shouldn't let anyone else know. In order to get there, we had to drive through the sugar cane fields, to the end of a dirt road, find the path along the ocean, and eventually cross a small river heading inland. The next afternoon we were on our way to this magical place. Heading inland along the river and through the thicket of greens, we suddenly stumbled across the opening of the cave. Right in front of us opened the dark mouth of the tunnel.

Bending down, we inched our way through the tunnel. The darkness felt ominous, and the wet, musty smell of the walls gave me chills. I didn't like the darkness, and my imagination grew quite creative on this canvas of blackness. Finally, in front of us I saw the dim light seeping in through an opening. The tunnel ended in an amphitheater-like cave, encircling us, opening to the sky. A stately banyan tree stood in the middle with wild roosters sitting and crowing in the branches.

Here, Hawaiians had out-waited their enemies in the distant past. The old history was still perceivable in the walls, which had served as a natural protection and hideout. It was nearing sunset and we had little time to explore the inside of the cave. Toward the back was an opening that led past what looked like an altar into the depth of the caverns. It looked ominous to me.

We still had to set up our tent before nightfall and decided against any further exploration. In the dim light of the setting sun we ate some cold tamales and soon crawled into our tent. As special as this place could be in the daytime, I was not thrilled by the prospect of us being there alone at night. In the presence of other tents at previous campsites I felt safe, but as the evening sky darkened, our tent here was a lonely refuge.

Snuggling up to one another we lay in the tent talking about impressions and thoughts we had in this place. Now and then we would fall silent and listen to the crickets chirping in the night-covered trees.

Suddenly I heard steps. Tip, tap, tip, tap. My heart leaped. I didn't think angels could make sounds on the ground. There it was again, plip, plap. My mind reeled. "Calm down, Ilona," I told myself. "You need to have your emotions a bit more under control."

I tried to calm myself, but still my heart pounded. Nothing really happened, but there was a trail of sounds going from the top of the tent along the side and across the front.

The anxious feeling made my imagination reel, and I got the strange idea that we were going to get picked up by a spaceship that night. Something in the air made me feel like we were going to have some kind of visitation. In anticipation, I snuggled up closer to Don. I loved feeling his body against mine. With my legs wrapped around his and his arms around me, I was flooded with warm feelings.

Although Don drifted off into dreamland easily, I remained alert for some time. When I did fall asleep I had a very vivid dream.

I was at a sandy beach on a bright, sunny day, and I stood

naked in the sun. As I stepped onto a rock, the waves started lapping at my feet, and I could sense the energy of the sun beaming through my body. Suddenly a dolphin swam up to me. I was either floating at that point or standing on a rock with my toes in the water when the dolphin came and touched my left toe with its beak.

As soon as he or she touched my toe, a beam of energy shot straight up my leg through my spine and out through the top of my head. I was electrified, stunned! A loud sound exploded straight through me, filling me with an intense light. This brilliant beam of light took me into another dimension for a brief moment and flooded my entire system with information at a speed faster than any thought could be. Charged by this intense light I bolted awake instantaneously.

This dream had been so intense that I felt like I had been initiated. The dolphin in my dream knew what it was doing. As I lay awake, breathing deeply now, I felt as if this dream was part of the calling of the dolphins. It may have been hard for me to find them in the external world, but inwardly the dolphins left no doubt that they could find me.

The next morning I told Don about my dream. The atmosphere was almost holy in this amphitheater. We both were moved by the dream. The inner worlds and the outer worlds were blending more and more. Though this experience was "only" a dream, we felt the impact to be perfectly real.

As we lay in the early morning mist, I heard the same sound as the night before. Tip, tap. We both sat up quickly and peeked out of our tent from behind the flap. A row of frogs was busily hopping back the same way they had come the night before. Now, in the dawn of light, the sounds were not menacing, but rather were greetings of a new day awaiting us.

17

It felt great to wake up so close to the ground. The sounds of the birds and the moist, earthy smells stimulated a sense of magic in me.

As we meditated together in the early morning light, I thanked the dolphins for dream-traveling with me. Inwardly I felt completely restructured and rejuvenated, and all this had happened on land, in dreamtime, not even in the water!

Our first week had ended with an amazing dream experience, and I was grateful. Would swimming with the dolphins in the water be as thrilling as my dream had been? For now I was content to have had some sign of a dolphin connection.

Days passed. Beautiful nature filled our senses, and we loved being surrounded by the elements, but I was starting to miss people of like mind. That morning in my meditation I longed for deeper soul connections. Breathing gently, I began rising higher and higher over the island in my imagination. Floating above the island I felt like I was becoming more and more light-filled, much like being part of the clouds. In this inner state I asked if there might be a bright Being on the island whom it would be beneficial to meet. As I scanned the island in my inner vision I saw a brilliant light shining on the eastern slopes of the central mountain, not too far away from the little town called Kapaa. My spirit rejoiced in this Being's light as we connected in a dimension outside the constraints of time and space. Here, we created a meeting as real as any meeting would be in the physical.

It was promising to think that we might meet a being of Light, and I told Don of my inner vision. After we packed up our tent, we bid the banyan tree farewell and thanked the amphitheater for having protected us for the night. Soon we made our way back along the river bank, crossing the small river as it met the ocean. It had been quite a night, and we hoped to see dolphins in the physical world soon.

On the way to Kapaa we stopped at a hidden accumulation of old, rundown buildings that turned out to be galleries and art stores of the alternative kind. I found myself wandering into a book store and soon discovered a book called *Call of the Dolphins*, by Lana Miller. I was thrilled. I was sure the dolphin world was talking to me.

While Don was driving I started reading out loud from the book, and more quickly than I anticipated we arrived in Kapaa. On the main road we found an artistic looking restaurant, called "Gecko's." We wandered in and made ourselves comfortable in a corner. The late afternoon sun streamed through the windows as we kept reading in our new book and nibbling on tasty treats.

Suddenly I caught the glance of a pair of brilliant blue eyes looking over at us. These eyes belonged to a blond man in his thirties. He was deciphering the title to our book, and as he did he started coming toward us. His blond hair and blue eyes made him look rather angelic.

"Are you interested in dolphins?" he asked in a warm tone. What an understatement!

"Yes, very much so," I answered sensing this being's light emanating from his heart.

Vaguely he reminded me of an inner guide, Go Pal Das,

with whom I had worked for the last few years. In a dream, he once appeared as my inner mentor with brilliant blue eyes, blond hair, and an intense emanation of love flowing from his heart.

"My name is Paul," he introduced himself. I smiled. As I looked at him I could feel the overlapping of the inner guide whom I had worked with and the outer being named Paul. My heart started to open wide, and I noticed I was becoming a bit concerned. Such strong feelings could lead to more than attraction, and I needed to stay aware.

Don happily took to Paul right away too, and we all got involved talking about dolphins. He told us where he had swum with them and how we also might be able to do so. He told us of a secret beach frequented by dolphins.

"I can take you there and we could spend an afternoon together," he offered.

"What a wonderful offer," I thought, "just the kind of vacation we were hoping to have—finding bright people who would go with us to hidden, tourist-free places!" We agreed to meet the following morning.

"Was it my inner asking during the morning meditation that brought us to meet this being?" I wondered. He certainly had the same brightness I had seen in my morning meditation. I marveled at the higher order of coordination. If I had not perceived the inner connection, I easily could have considered our afternoon meeting with Paul a coincidence at best, or perhaps fate. Many dimensions are at work to create the final results in the three-dimensional world, and much of the inner work stays hidden from view.

The following morning we met Paul and some friends

of his, two women and one man. Finally we arrived at the secret beach. It was quite a hike! Almost sliding down a ravine, we came out of the forest near the mouth of a freshwater river. The dark green of the trees gave way to the brilliant blue sparkle of the ocean. It took us another forty-five minutes to hike along the beach before we stretched out on our blankets on the soft white sand. It was a free beach, no clothing required, and it felt wonderful to be naked.

After we settled down and exchanged with everyone in our little group what we each were about, I suggested a game. We would all sit in a circle and quiet our minds, feeling the gentle weight of our bodies on the sand. Enjoying the sun shining through the leaves of the palm trees and hearing the wind rustling the leaves, we were to go slowly to a place of peace and beauty . . . I felt like I was already there. My inner place of peace was very similar to this one—a white beach in paradise with a soft breeze and sunshine, waves rolling onto the shore, and palm trees overhead . . .

I said in a gentle voice, " . . . And from a distance you start noticing a brilliant being coming toward you, . . . a radiant being! And as this being comes closer and closer to you . . . you realize it is you in your fullest potential, in your highest expression of who you really are."

I could feel the impact of our imagination. Waves of awe surged through me . . . "What qualities does your fullest potential have? Take note of three qualities," I continued.

I saw great wisdom and love emanating from my full potential, a celestial angel.

" . . . And then say your name to yourself, and as you do,

you slip inside this being, your full potential. Notice how it feels to be fully realized . . . Feel your true inner nature filling all your cells, flooding you with information, with brilliance and love . . . and as you do, see the person sitting across from you in his or her full potential as well . . . Which colors do you see in them? What qualities do you notice?"

Since Paul sat opposite me in the circle, I chose to see him in his full potential. He transfigured to look like my inner guide Go Pal Das. Increasing love flowed from him, and he was radiant beyond any words . . . Bluish-golden light surrounded him, and in an inviting gesture he asked me to join with him in my inner light body . . . We started spiraling upward, as though we were traveling through layers and layers of light, through levels of consciousness . . .

With each passing layer we became increasingly more filled with light and spanned across the entire inner space, slowly beginning to blend and become one. As both our fields united deeper and deeper, I felt an immensity of love flooding through me. We burst through one last layer of blending into oneness, beyond which I could no longer tell us apart. Rather, we became an ecstatically exploding fountain of light.

I felt I had entered God and I surrendered all my love to the "Oneness-of-All-that-Is," letting go and letting this Oneness traverse the expanse of the universe . . . I felt I was One with God, the Source of "All-that-Is" . . .

Information flooded through me, and it was as though, through my own surrender, I was able to transcend any previous limits and nourish my soul with a new level of learning. I felt at once no longer "myself" and was at the same time aware that my beingness could and would coalesce into a self-identity anytime it was needed. It is our willingness to let go of our sense of self that enables us to become more of what we truly are.

Then an image-message from Paul came floating into my mind. "Let this energy come back around and touch the soles of your feet, like a fountain flowing back onto itself, refreshed with the memory of God, Love and Oneness."

Tears flowed from my eyes, and my heart felt like bursting. The ecstasy filled all time and space, as I knew it, and Heaven was all around me. "Let this love envelop the earth and see it flowing up and around like the fountain in you. Let our love nourish the world you touch," the voice continued. "And one more thing, please remember that you are in touch with an inner state now. Please remember not to attach our oneness and love to my personality, to my body. You can enter into this state with anyone who can surrender their soul into God . . . I am the inner one you have come to know and love. *Your task is to live in Heaven on Earth.* This will inspire everyone around you who is open to living in Heaven now . . ."

Feeling the joy flooding through my cells, I slowly came back to my senses. What a journey! Don and I joined in Oneness like this as often as we could raise our vibration high enough to experience it, and I considered it the main staple of our ecstatic relationship. Here I had the joy of a full experience with another being I felt I had known internally for a long time.

As we all started to open our eyes, I could still see in my

mind the light body surrounding Paul. We took turns sharing in the group what we each had experienced, and we soon started looking at each other with different eyes. Don was glowing with love; blue sparkles filled his eyes and the air around him. I felt so open to Don and knew that the fertile soil of our relationship was nourished by our love and our surrender to Spirit, and upon this rich soil we were able to learn and grow.

I was curious to know what Paul had experienced. He had a very similar journey to mine and shared his experience openly with the group. Since it had been filled with such universal energy, it didn't feel like it was an exclusive experience between him and me, but rather it served as an inspiration to each one of us to realize that the boundaries of our available experiences were far more fluid than we often knew.

It was amazing to everyone that we got so much information about each other in such a short time, as if we were all skilled psychic readers. By seeing each other in our imagination at the highest potential, we also saw many other details about each other.

All information in the universe is accessible if we can commune and somehow create a resonance with it. Through the use of imagery we create a bridge, or a doorway, and share the same space with whatever we are looking at or inquiring about.

The light that filled our little group made it truly look like we were on an island in paradise. Although we looked for our dolphins all day, none came around, so we just played in the ocean waves.

At one point Don and I lay under the trees by ourselves. Don was rubbing my feet, and I enjoyed feeling the wind blow gently all around my naked skin. We talked about the otherworldly light everyone had taken on, about love in the inner dimensions, and about how union is so puzzling. Loving union of our souls seems to be filled with so much joy and ecstasy, and at the same time it can stimulate our desire for sexual union as well.

Yet, when the desire for sexual union is acted upon outside a monogamous relationship, it can often turn into a struggle of choices, of either/or and this may destroy the deep sense of trust and vulnerability that a couple has taken time to develop. The challenge is to realize the naturalness of the desire for union, which wants to express itself on all levels from spiritual to sexual, and at the same time have the maturity to realize both our human limitations and the innate nature of reality, being separate while desiring oneness.

The feeling in the inner dimensions is that the whole universe is based on the all-inclusive, cohesive energy of Love and Union. Without this, all creation would fly apart. But our three-dimensional personal self lives in a dual reality, in a realm of separation. On the one hand there is the ecstatic experience of Oneness, and on the other there is the desire to remain as a separate unit of identity, whether expressed as a personal self or collectively as a relationship, family, or nation.

Trying to reconcile the limitation of a three-dimensional form with an infinite Soul is a challenge, a paradox to be embraced.

18

Later that day Don and I went back to our campsite. "High" from seeing the true beauty of ourselves and others, we started preparing our evening meal. There were many campers that night and pots banged, children laughed, and families ate together. We were in the midst of what felt like tribal living.

Most everyone had spent the day under the open sky, and I wondered if that in itself changes people. How much does the exposure to the natural elements, the cosmos above our heads, alter our minds? I know whenever I have gone backpacking, after just a few days my eyes look so much wilder, more alive. Upon returning to "civilization," the sight of traffic lights and skyrises makes me shriek.

Later in the evening some people gathered, playing guitar and singing songs. Don and I took a walk along the beach as the stars were shining and we stopped here and there to listen in. Eyes were sparkling in the firelight, and we felt at ease with this "non-ordinary" way of life.

Later on we settled down in our tent and snuggled up together. I thought about how we had wanted to meet with dolphins and yet had not been able to. Why was it so difficult? Were our "vibes" so dense that no dolphin wanted to be close to us? Had we chosen the wrong island or the wrong time or what? As I asked myself these questions I suddenly had an idea. What if I started talking in my inner mind to the dolphins who surely must be swimming not too far from our tent?! We were in line with the shore of the secret beach, and maybe I could send my thoughts out into the waters.

I sat up in order to better focus my mind and moved into a pinpoint of light. Slowly all other noises faded away as the impressions of the watery environment started to swirl around me. This was the world in which these majestic beings lived, a buoyant world in which gravity was almost nonexistent, where sounds traveled so much faster than in air, and where seeing was much farther down the list of priorities.

In my mind I reached out to the dolphin pod as I imagined them to be. "When in doubt make it up!" I remembered. In my minds eye I "saw" the pod swimming together, and yet I felt like I was just observing them. "Maybe they have someone like a top dolphin," I mused. I pretended in my imagination to send a greeting of love to this being. Sure enough, it felt like I reached someone on the other end of the greeting. It was an older being, stronger and quicker minded than the other pod members, at least as I perceived them.

"I am a leader figure so to speak, and I'm representing our clan," I heard in my mind. I felt awed. This being really responded to me, at least in my mind, and by now I had learned that my imagination was often closer to reality than I dared to believe. I sent out the image-message that I wanted to meet with the dolphins a.s.a.p., if, and whenever, it was appropriate, of course. At this point I felt like there was an instantaneous response from the leader dolphin that it felt a sense of kinship with us and would like to meet with us, but it first wanted to check with the others.

It was as though I were watching this scene from a short

distance. The new information about Don's and my desire to meet with the dolphin pod spread among them. Some were leery, some disinterested, and some very open to the idea. Eventually a consensus was met. "Come and meet us at the 'secret beach' at 8:45 A.M. in the morning," the lead dolphin communicated to me. "We'll be there!" he ended the conversation.

"Roger, over," is what I almost expected to hear in my mind, as I found myself sitting in our tent, wondering if what had just occurred was real or not. "Well, I'd better tell Don about our first official date with the dolphins," I thought to myself and had to laugh. An imaginary appointment. Good thing it was with dolphins. Had I imagined a human on the other side I might not have taken my imagery experience so seriously. Somehow I had more trust in the telepathic ability of dolphins.

Just as I was telling Don about my internal interlude and snuggling up to him under the warm blankets on the hard ground, I heard the first drops of rain hitting our tent. Luckily we had nestled our tent next to a tree and wouldn't get soaked that night. "Oh, no," Don moaned, "dolphins hate murky waters, and I've heard that the water runoff from the mountains can make the ocean murky after a rain! That's certainly not the best time to see dolphins!"

But we had made the agreement with them, and sleeping was the only thing we could do at this time. "We also don't have an alarm clock!" I sighed. What a downer after such a great meditation! I hoped that we would wake up really early.

The rain sent everyone into their tents, which reduced the noise level of the campground, and soon we fell asleep.

19

The next morning loud noises woke us up. Kids were squealing and parents were preparing breakfast. It had stopped raining, and the sun was breaking through the morning clouds. We had no idea what time it was, so we got up swiftly, made our breakfast consisting of oats, guava juice, and a papaya, and then we packed everything into our rental car. It was 7:30 A.M. according to our car clock, which left us exactly enough time to get to our potential rendezvous with the dolphins.

We drove quietly to the "secret beach" and packed our flippers, masks, snorkels, beach mats, towels, and food in some bags. Once we made it down to the beach, it would take us another forty-five minutes to walk to the specific spot the dolphins had shown me in my meditation. "Yeah, right!" I thought.

Soon we were trotting through the sand, enjoying the waves lapping at the beach. After half an hour of walking, our gear got heavy, especially since our feet were sinking into the deep, white sand with every step we took. Scanning the ocean we watched for dolphins, but none were in sight.

Finally, we reached our spot and dropped everything. Was it worth it, I wondered? We really were trying our best to connect with the dolphins. Did they know that? Suddenly someone pointed to the waves in front of us. "See the dorsal fins?" someone said, pointing to something invisible to my eyes. "I see something. It looks like part of a wave, like little black dots, that are hard to distinguish from the waves,"

Don said excitedly to me. "Yes, there, I see a whole bunch of them!"

I was excited! Quickly I ran over to a man who was wearing a watch. "Excuse me, what time is it?" I asked. "It's 8:45," he answered, puzzled by why I would care to know the time in this tropical paradise. I ran back to Don and told him. "See, they did come for their appointment."

We jumped up and down!! What a treat. Trusting my inner imagery had worked. Perhaps the dolphins and I had really communicated, even though I felt kind of silly.

We were trying to get our snorkeling gear on quickly when we noticed that the dolphins were heading back out of the bay. "What are they doing?" I wondered. "Did they just come in to say, yes, we kept our date and now we're off?"

This was hardly the kind of rendezvous I had hoped for. As I reviewed my inner session with them, I remembered that it had been a bit difficult to reach a consensus from all the group members. Indeed, the agreement was about meeting at a specific time, which did not imply it was going to take place in the water. I hadn't sent the image of being "face to face" with them, even though I thought my desire was obvious.

Without dolphins in the water, the ocean didn't have much appeal to me. I was actually a bit scared by the depth of the water, by the waves, and by the unruliness of the ocean in general.

As I thought about the ambivalence I had about the water I overheard someone saying that the dolphins usually came back after a couple of hours. Hoping that this would be true, Don and I settled onto the beach near some palm trees and relaxed. I loved to lay on the sand and look up into the sky, watching the palms blow back and forth, giving me a feeling of awe for nature and God's creation.

I felt it was good that we had some time to calm down and open ourselves to the rhythms and beauty of the ocean waves and nature surrounding us. We let go of our daily concerns with each breath we took in this tropical paradise.

A couple of hours went by. As soon as we saw the first group of fins popping out of the waves we jumped up. Yes, indeed, the man had been right; the dolphins were coming back.

Now I understood the reason for their sudden departure after only five minutes at the beach in the morning. Had they hung out in the bay I could have arrived late for our appointment and would never have noticed the difference. By their arriving at 8:45 A.M. and disappearing at 8:50 A.M. I had confirmation that I had understood the dolphins correctly. They had kept their agreement!

Excitedly we got our fins and snorkels ready. This was it!! Our first time out with the dolphins! My hands and legs were shaking as I tried to hurry. Don was faster than I and started walking ahead of me. "Wait!" I shouted, "I'm afraid to go into the water by myself here."

We had gone snorkeling, but only in protected areas, and certainly not in very deep water. As we arrived at the water's edge we spit into our masks to keep them from fogging up and then rinsed them out.

Soon the water reached my thighs, and it was cold! But the dolphins were here! The waves were not the smallest either, as the rain and wind from the night before had stirred up the ocean. Nevertheless we jumped in, along with a few other people who had the same desire to meet the dolphins.

Since the dolphin pod was continuously moving, we had to keep looking for them. The water got deeper and deeper, and the waves around us were quite high, such that we couldn't always see where the dolphins were headed. As I paddled with my flippers, trying to swim in the right direction, I suddenly felt a deep sense of trust come over me. I let go of struggling to swim or trying to find the dolphins, and I simply let myself be carried by the waves. Bobbing up and down in the deep water surprisingly didn't bother me anymore.

This feeling of being at home in the water was in such contrast to how I felt earlier that it really struck me. I felt at home in the water! As I put my head back underwater, I couldn't see very far—maybe one body's length— as the water was murky, but I heard the dolphins' sonar for the first time. Their calls were short and high pitched, sometimes in close succession, like pearls on a string. Some of them seemed to be aimed at me and touched my body like bubbles.

The dolphins were here, right around us, and although I could not see them I felt high! The sound of the sonar seemed to touch me, yet my familiar sense of sight could not confirm the dolphins' presence. Then I lifted my head out of the water, and there, maybe fifteen feet away, a baby spinner dolphin jumped out of the water, splashing back down into the waves. What a beautiful sight! They were probably all around us, and yet we could not see them.

Well, the dolphins surely could see us, both inside and out. It is said that dolphins can sense and view a person's emotional state with their sonar. If my meditation the prior evening and my dreams had any reality to them, the dolphins would know us inside out better than we dared to think. I felt at home!

20

That night I had another dream. I was swimming in the ocean near the shore, floating along on the surface of the waves, when a dolphin came swimming toward me. This dolphin snuggled up to me, and I felt safe in his close presence. How I loved it! His skin was very smooth as he brushed by me, and I had the feeling an eternal friend had come back to see me. Suddenly I noticed how the " air" around him, which was really the water, started glowing brightly with luminous light. Simultaneously I started feeling more alert and open. At this point there was a group of six or seven dolphins surrounding me. And as they were forming a circle around me, the first dolphin mentally told me that they were going to change the vibrational structure of my cells, and in this way they would restructure my being. As he told me this, I felt the circle of dolphins closing in on me, sending rays of light and sonar into the essence of my very core.

I felt so exhilarated! Their intent to restructure me was very clear, with no doubts tainting their work. Later, as I awoke and reflected on the night's excursion, I had no doubt the experience was real! I believe the dolphins really manifested into the dimension of my dream in order to work with me that night. Slowly, I was starting to catch on to the possibility that dolphins were skilled inter-dimensional travelers, and it was no wonder so many artists depict dolphins and whales swimming among the stars in outer-space. They seem to feel at home in the expanse of water, air, and vacuum, as well as in the dreamtime space, using different parts of themselves to travel in these domains.

What if they had learned to access subtle realms of existence much more consciously than humans? Perhaps their communication to me about meeting at a specific time was a literal appointment, much like making an appointment on the phone would be for us.

If that were true, I had to take my imaginings more seriously. Any negative imagery could be a palpable reality. I pondered my habits. Sometimes I ran whole movies in my mind about a possible sad outcome for a story, starring me as the saddest victim. I decided to be more vigilant about my thoughts. Part of me in a slightly subtler form would appreciate not being the peon of my negative imagery.

As if in answer to my new understanding, I felt the presence of my dolphin friend within me. "That's right," he nudged me. "We have developed nonmaterial skills, like raising our awareness levels to include many of the realities that humans, as a general rule, have not yet awakened to. Ecstasy is one of the by-products. When we send out our sonar pulses, we can alter cellular frequencies that affect physical and emotional health. That is why humans feel so elevated after being in our presence."

I recalled having heard about people in pain becoming either partially or completely pain free after swimming with dolphins. I have also talked to people whose tumors have disappeared after swimming with dolphins, which they attributed to the effects of the dolphins' sonar. But the most often heard comment was that dolphins were like superior psychotherapists, stimulating a person's growth and development from wherever he or she was at.

In my mind I kept accepting that the information I perceived was coming from the dolphin. "Anyone who is traveling the same frequencies as we do will become aware of our presence and will notice the coincidences between the inner and the outer worlds," he finished, leaving me in a soft bubble of joy.

"Imagination is real," I kept thinking. Who had put this thought into my mind? Had the dolphins really started to restructure me? And if so, then according to what plan, in which direction? Somehow I felt secure, like I did when I was bobbing up and down in the waves with the dolphins all around, even though I couldn't see them . . .

21

Heaven on Earth... Heaven on Earth. This thought kept pulsating through my mind and heart as we spent our last few days on Kauai. I remember the second day we swam with the dolphins.

Another couple visiting Kauai on their honeymoon had joined us in our quest. They had found a guardian water angel too, yet another one with blond hair and blue eyes. This former dive instructor was all too willing to help us get into the waves at the right time and help us find the rhythms of the dolphins.

This time it seemed so much easier. Having his help greatly enhanced our experience. He knew what signs to look for, and also knew the cycles by which the dolphins lived, and so the four of us took to him like ducklings to a mother duck. At one point he mentioned that dolphins enjoy feeling sensual excitement coming from people and tend to show extra interest when it is present. All four of us felt like we might have just found the right kind of bait for them...

Lulled by the waves around us we hung out on the surface of the water in pairs, each of the two pairs separated by a short distance. What we didn't realize was that the distance between us did not act as a wall. Our underwater attempts to arouse our partners were clearly visible to anyone looking through his or her mask, especially since all the mud from the rain had settled.

I saw the other couple floating naked in the waves,

caressing each other and showing visible signs of arousal. Needless to say, they could see us too. A world without walls. The night's darkness is only our human boundary, but not the dolphin's. Dolphins see primarily through the use of their sonar, and there is virtually no way to hide. Even internal states of thought and emotion appear like an open book to them.

Imagine if we had no way to hide, no privacy as we know it, with our thoughts completely in the open. What would it be like if everything we do, feel, and think was open to others?

I remember a woman lecturer who once conveyed a lesson she learned from aborigines in Australia. "Everyone can be telepathic," she had said. "It is to the degree that we have nothing to hide, no lies, no secrets to keep that the world around us becomes permeable, see-through-able. It is our own lies, small as they may be, that build the walls through which we cannot see. If we clear the windows of our own perception, we will see and hear the whispers of each other's thoughts."

Here, underwater, I felt the impact of how our lives would be different if we had no walls. Maybe that was the lesson for this morning, because despite our good show, our sexual bait didn't work. Deep inside me, however, I realized some changes. I felt more trusting, more in awe of the beauty in everyone and everything. I felt like I belonged. Although I had been brought up to keep my sexual life private, I actually enjoyed seeing the beauty of the caressing dance of the other couple. The absence of walls didn't seem to make us feel uncomfortable, but at the same time we also stayed was gazing into the light surrounding our world, I saw my inner guide entering my field of perception. A supernatural sense surrounded him, his immense love flowing through me.

With an intense magnetic charge between us, I felt us becoming a fountain of Light together. As if by the force of our union, we both rushed up and up as though we were flying into higher realms. Finally a serene level of white light expanded before us, and I could no longer "see" us as I had before. Instead we were "One," and understanding filled my heart.

It was as though I were shown how, here at this level of reality, we are no longer divided into lower and higher, but instead can feel the goodness of each being and see into the heart of each soul.

I saw the energy around the souls of business people and of some politicians, and also saw the pattern of learning they were facing. All the learning seemed to head in one direction—letting the love that is all around us, and clearly visible here, enter our hearts.

As I saw this Light-Love mixture enter the beings at whom I was looking, I also saw how they would make different choices in their physical world as a result of love filling their essence.

"As you are willing to see this potential around each person you meet and see his or her true heart, you are actually helping the Love become part of each person's life and yours," my inner guide transmitted.

I knew these thoughts to be part of my learning here and could feel the truth impacting me deeply. If I applied this to my daily life, it meant that I could create a change in "my" world, which might reflect itself in my personal or global experience. Apparently, my inner acknowledgment of another's love and light potential had the effect of creating favorable changes.

The dolphins had something to do with this vision, and my inner preparation prior to coming to Hawaii had enabled me to see the potential in people. The Time Traveler had been part of this unfolding picture as well.

As Don and I slowly came back to our senses, we looked at each other for a long time in silence. It was as if we were living on many different levels. On one level we were humans; on another level we looked like angels to each other, moving higher yet, we could no longer tell where we started or where we ended. Bliss and Oneness were showering upon us from all around. Whenever we went into this realm, I noticed that our physical life became much more harmonious, and we were much more in love.

I understood that this way of seeing one another had to do with the feeling of being "in love." The magic of "falling in love" is simply a way of sharing higher dimensions in oneness together. Many people could actually learn *how* to *be in love* and be in that state again and again.

Contentedly we fell asleep.

23

The next day we were scheduled to meet a couple that friends in Seattle had recommended we visit. They were interested in the SE-5, and we had brought one with us to show them.

Languidly we made our way to the northern end of the island to visit with Bill and Lanaya. As we arrived, we pulled into a luxurious tropical world. There we found a million-dollar home set on a ravine with a tropical river below and surrounded by a garden filled with flowers of all kinds and colors. The smells wafting toward us made us feel welcome instantaneously.

Lanaya, being pregnant, greeted us in her yellow jumpsuit that stretched tightly over her belly. The house had been cared for meticulously, and the many carvings in the beams and wood posts gave it an artistic flair.

Our introduction went smoothly, and since we had a common interest we quickly warmed up to one another. As we were sitting around a wooden table at the bay window, Don and I kept looking at this woman. Didn't we know her from somewhere? Finally we found the remarkable answer. A year earlier she had come to our house in Seattle as a woman in distress.

She had come to visit us with a friend who was interested in some of our instruments. We had been giving free demonstrations at our house, and this particular day her friend was trying one out, having Don explain all the uses.

Lanaya was not into the "techno-stuff" so she and I had gone outside to sit on our front porch swing. As we were swaying in the gentle late-autumn wind, our conversation soon deepened, and it became obvious that she needed help. Her life was far less than desirable. She was with an unreliable man who barely made a living, and she felt that she was not expressing her purpose in life. She wasn't coming close to living any of her dreams.

Her visit occurred only a short while after our training with the Time Traveler, and I was willing to try my newly learned skills.

Linda, her name at the time, was willing to give it a try, and so I guided her gently to trust her body's knowledge. She slowed down enough in her thinking to give her inner wisdom a chance to speak. Our body speaks the truth if we are willing to listen and if we can learn to decipher its messages. Her feelings centered in her belly and in her heart. She felt downtrodden, not daring to dream anymore, because she had lost the belief that she deserved any joy.

As we worked through many layers, she transformed this feeling into a vision of wanting to contribute to life, of wanting to give the gift of love to others in whatever form it came to her. A radiant sun was the symbol of her strength, and a rainbow represented walking the path of vision and love.

These two images helped her regroup the neurological pathways of her past memories of unworthiness, and if she stayed connected to these new images in her mind, she would soon be walking a different path in life. I was moved. Not only did everything go smoothly—even though it took a bit longer than I had originally thought I could handle—I also felt a shift inside myself. As she went through the process of listening to her body, allowing the feelings to become images, then transforming them into their deepest desire so they became her allies instead of enemies, I felt the transformation touch a part of my soul as well. It was as though with each healing I assisted, part of me was healing too.

As we discovered this past history together at her home on Kauai, we were all stunned. The difference in her life was so staggering that I had not recognized her. Silently the universe had given me a gift, letting me see the visible transformation of her life after we had worked together. The credit goes to Life.

This experience strengthened my resolve to continue helping people learn this method, to integrate it over time, and to show anyone willing to learn how they could help others.

Lanaya and her new husband had opened a bed and breakfast here on Kauai where Lanaya also offered massage. This was her way of sharing her love and her gifts with people. The house had several little cottages on the property when they bought it, and in one of these cottages she gave massages. Here we would sleep the coming night.

The rest of the day we continued to play with the SE-5 and talk of all the miracles we had experienced. Don and I love to learn for ourselves and then help others learn to shift possibilities in our so-called "solid" world. In our journeying we have found that everything points in one direction: becoming more and more a co-creator of Love and

Heaven on Earth in God's universe.

We are creating our own realities all the time, consciously or unconsciously, and we can learn to become increasingly a mirror of beauty and love. I call our earthly experience as humans "Angels in Training on Earth."

24

We spent a wonderful night in the little healing temple that Lanaya had created and took a fresh outdoor shower the next morning. It was so exhilarating to shower naked among the trees in fresh air that I vowed, if possible, to someday have an outdoor shower too.

After breakfast, we bid farewell to Bill and Lanaya and went to an extraordinary snorkeling spot called "Tunnels." Vacationing is fun because we meet so many different kinds of people and do things that in the normal rhythm of responsibilities we don't do. Hawaii is more carefree than most places. The environment alone makes one need less protection in the form of clothing and shelter, and meeting people is very easy.

By now, however, Don and I needed time just for the two of us, and we spent the next day snorkeling, reading in the dolphin book, and enjoying camping near the beach at night. The following day we hiked up the Napali coast and were thrilled by the pure turquoise color of the ocean.

Soon the vacation would come to an end, and we started feeling restless, ready to do something. It became clear to me that pure free time without some form of expression would soon overload a human system. I understood how so many people who do nothing, or create nothing, often by default alter their perception through drugs or watching television. We met quite a few people who watched two or more videos a day here in Hawaii, since they had nothing else to do. After a while the brain gets lazy and loves the canned moving-picture stories. Instead of creating their own stories that would help express their own beauty, many have become addicted to the moving-picture show.

Most people think that they are the master of their choices, that they "want" to watch this or that. Many do not notice how subtly addictive the pictures are to their brains, how one hour per week turns into many more. Nor do they notice the drain of energy, the immense amount of time the subconscious mind spends working over the stories, trying to digest these fast-moving picture-meals.

Yet if one does not give in to this kind of ready-made fodder for the brain, one's mind will get busy creating its own picture show. With the right focus, it will then start manifesting miracles in the outer world. But one needs to know how to talk to that part of the mind, how to work with it effectively, how to access the secret trail into the super-conscious mind.

The Time Traveler and the dolphins were pointing the way for us. Imagery was the key, no matter how "old" this knowledge was.

It is "being" in this imagery-rich way of life that makes the difference between living in Heaven on Earth . . . or not.

During the previous afternoon at Tunnels, I had been reading the book *The Call of the Dolphins*. In it Lana Miller describes her experiences of meeting dolphins and people who had worked with them. This afternoon I read about Roberta Quist-Goodman, who had worked with John Lilly,

Wisdom of the Dolphins

the first famous American dolphin researcher. The movie, *Day of the Dolphin* seems to have been written as a result of his work.

Roberta had been working with him on a dolphin release program for the two dolphins Joe and Rosie. John Lilly had captured the dolphins in 1980 from the Gulf of Mexico with the solemn promise that if he were permitted to catch them, he would someday set them free. This required untraining the dolphins because once dolphins become used to being fed they have a hard time relearning to catch their own food. This reminded me of the human brains that love being fed picture stories.

Roberta had been working with Joe and Rosie for three to four years, doing everything from scrubbing the tanks to playing intricate games to helping them unlearn rehearsed behavior.

One of the stories that Lana Miller recounted especially impressed me. Here it is:

Roberta thought of an experiment to test whether Joe was really as telepathic as she had felt he was. She wanted to determine how much this was the case. She wondered whether some of her subtle body language might have given him and Rosie clues as to what she was thinking, and thereby skewing her impressions, especially about Joe's telepathic ability. In order to eliminate any chance of her body giving clues, she devised the following experiment.

At home she thought up a phrase that would describe being a dolphin and it was: "Feeling water life thing." She had used the symbols from a system called "The language of space." It has thirty-three letters, and each of the letters has a symbolic meaning. For each of the words in her phrase she projected the following images.

She first pictured in her mind the concept of "feeling" as half a heart. Second was "water," which she pictured as just that: water. The third was "life," which she pictured as a leaf, and the fourth was "thing," which she pictured as a big dot. One evening she sent these pictures in the same sequence to Joe, who seemed the most attuned to her mind and more conscious than Rosie.

The next morning she walked up to the pool where Joe was to be for the day and sent out the thought "Hi there, anything new?" As soon as she asked, he swam towards her, then headed off swimming a half heart. At the finish he came zooming back as if to ask, "Did you get it?" Roberta did get it, and noticed how similar it was to her image the night before, but did not expect anything more of him.

To her surprise, Joe next dashed over to Roberta and squirted water at her. "Hmm, could that be *water* as I had imaged?" she wondered. Apparently Joe was happy with her level of understanding because next he turned over onto his side and waved with his pectoral fin. This fin had the shape of a leaf, thin at the tip, rounding out softly at the bottom.

Roberta was absolutely thrilled. "Could it be," she wondered, "that he received all of my thoughts and received them accurately?"

Apparently with glee, Joe dashed off over to a black inner tube and poked his beak through the middle. "What is this supposed to mean?" she wondered. "Was it the dot I had pictured? Certainly it was the closest thing in sight to the big dot," Roberta concluded.

This experiment proved to her beyond the slightest doubt that Joe had read her mind, had picked up the images and not in a vague way, but rather verbatim. Several trainers have noted that dolphins sometimes seem to do new "tricks" before they are shown how to do them. Rather, they seem to respond after the trainer has only imagined them.

There are also trainers who feel that dolphins are nothing more than smart animals, and they have ample stories to prove it. Roberta feels that often dolphins demonstrate to the trainer the exact fulfillment of the vision the trainer has of the dolphins' capacity. This is so true that with one trainer a dolphin was smart, instantaneously responsive, and telepathic. With another trainer the same dolphin was slow to learn, apparently dumb, and barely seemed to catch on to the meaning of the training signals.

A gift that Roberta feels she received from her years of contact with Joe and Rosie is that they taught her to deal with the situation at hand by making use of all possibilities, by deeply contacting her own ability to trust and showing her how to enter new dimensions.

25

I was fascinated! If dolphins, as Joe had shown, could read the thought images someone had sent him, then maybe my telepathic experiences with dolphins were indeed as solidly real as I had hoped they were.

I thought of our "appointment" the first time at the "secret beach," of the dreams I had shared with them, and of the saving of the whales after I dreamed that dolphins signaled me about the whale's distress.

What implications did this form of communication have? For one thing, it implied the existence of a real world that is outside the confines of the three dimensional world in which we think we live. Telepathy, although invisible to the physical eyes, points to the connection between the laws and energies that govern our physical experience. There are multiple dimensions in which we live daily that affect our everyday life, whether we are aware of them or not.

The next level of implication was much larger than I dared to think. My "whale/dolphin dream" in particular, in which the whales were rescued in waking reality somehow in tandem with my dream, hinted at a level of interaction of dimensions that is beyond the confines of linear time and outside of what we humans allow ourselves to believe in.

I became more and more convinced that interacting on the level of imagery creates real results in the world in which we live, even miles away from where we are. This implication alone carries with it much hope. The dreams and images we carry with us in our daily lives do make a difference. I was excited to think that I could spend time in these dimensions and help myself and others by daydreaming.

On a more physical level of communication, it has been surmised that dolphins can hold two conversations at once. For example, it is said that a dolphin can simultaneously communicate with a dolphin nearby and with another one five miles away.

"At least one species on this planet has developed a nervous system sophisticated enough to enter into realms of realities that are still beyond the scope and reach of most humans. We might do well to start learning from dolphins," I mused.

Our time alone refreshed us, and Don and I talked about the possibility of spending more time with the dolphins. Our next free time would be in June of the following year—maybe we could come back! We were excited at the thought.

With that in mind, we headed back toward civilization. Our first stop was at the health food store in Hanapepe. As we meandered through the store, with its wonderful smells of wholesome breads and treats, the glowing eyes of a tall woman caught my eyes. She exuded feelings of love for anyone crossing her path, and I marveled at her beauty of spirit. Within a few minutes we were talking about the beautiful spots to visit on Kauai. She and her partner had a bed and breakfast on Maui, and they told us about their Zodiac boat. They said if we came to visit them on Maui we probably could visit with dolphins there, too. Their price was so reasonable at twenty-five dollars a night that we decided to go to Maui in early summer of the following year.

Things were falling into place. Paul and his girlfriend kindly invited us to spend the last night at their house, and we gladly accepted the invitation and enjoyed a warm shower. The following morning we packed everything up and headed to the airport by mid-afternoon.

It had been a very rich time in every way, and the energy of the dolphins seemed to be building. I definitely had learned that dolphins challenge my fears and make me face those fears so that I could overcome them. They also helped me to realize that with patience and persistence I have the power to overcome my inner obstacles. I also started to realize that the exchanges that occur in the inner dimensions in the form of dreams or thought transmissions with dolphins were becoming reality. This inner communion was a way to have access to the dolphins' energy without ever touching water. Ecstasy was becoming a "new" frequency in our lives.

Soon we were once again flying high above the clouds, leaving the Hawaiian Islands behind us.

Seattle greeted us with its green trees, snow-peaked mountains, and misty rain. How I loved to breathe the air here! After so much time off, Don and I were looking forward to our work. We were in the process of building our home—a geodesic dome—on a North Pacific island an hour and a half north of Seattle.

Previously, our Time Traveler had offered to take us in as trainees, and we already had begun training with him. Soon we would pass on to others how to enter the dreamtime world and live in Heaven on Earth.

26

One night shortly after our return from Hawaii I received a very clear dream message. Don and I were to create a guided imagery tape that would allow people to enter into the world of Dolphin Consciousness.

I had just begun to write the script, and in preparation for writing the next section I sat down on our couch on a quiet afternoon to read in Lana Miller's book, *Call of the Dolphins*. By "coincidence" I read about how Lana Miller had traveled to a desert area near Sedona, Arizona, and had taken part in a guided imagery group herself. A woman there had created a guided-imagery journey to get in touch with dolphins and Lana Miller went on in her book to describe it somewhat like this: "You are slowly stepping into a pool of water . . . you notice a dolphin coming up to you, touching the right or left big toe and shooting a zapping beam of energy up your spine . . . you can feel it travel through your body and out the top of your head . . ."

"Wait a minute!" I thought, "I can't believe that someone has made a guided-imagery journey that is a complete replica of a vivid dream I recently had. The memory was still fresh enough to jolt my senses. In my dream I had been zapped with super high frequencies from the dolphin's sonar, and the whole experience had felt like an initiation. What was going on? Was there a deeper meaning to this coincidence?

Perhaps dolphins administer similar jolts of initiation to numerous people during dreams? Maybe it was something archetypal.

To find out more about the dolphins' intentions for me, I closed my eyes. By now I was convinced that any "fantasy experiences" I had with dolphins were real. I almost felt like my dolphin friend was floating in midair waiting for me. It was not a coincidence that I had just read about this journey. What were they doing? I wanted to find out!

In my mind I traveled to the same space where I pretended to see the dolphin waiting for me . . . There I saw a sphere of light surrounding myself and the floating dolphin . . . Slowly I expanded my feeling of understanding, "getting" the messages all at once as if in a thought ball . . . I sent a question to my inner dolphin friend about the meaning of the coincidence of my dream and the story in Lana Miller's book. Within a moment I got it. I understood the meaning to be something like this: "We want you to write your dream experience as part of your guided-imagery journey, just like the woman did in her book. We are communicating with you and anyone else who is focused enough, and you will find us inside."

It was a good thing the dolphins directed me so clearly, because in my belief system it was better to keep all inner experiences to myself. Mass-producing them was certainly not my first choice.

Since my dolphin guide and friend seemed to have an idea of what might do well on such a tape, I asked if it wanted something special to be said. As I looked with my inner vision, I saw the dolphin pointing its head out of the ocean waters into the sky. It nudged me to follow him to another world. Higher and higher we went, out among the stars . . . flying in unison . . . until we came to what looked like a watery planet. We dived into its atmosphere and spun down, around each other, into the deeper layers of the planet's waters . . . Immediately the dolphin took me to a vast meeting place of other beings who seemed to know my friend and guide very well.

Within moments the group of beings started forming a spiral around me, taking my conscious mind into a whirling spin, shifting my level and capacity of understanding to a super-conscious level . . . I started seeing a gridwork of light lines interconnecting, stretching around the globe of their planet . . . At nodal points, where two or more lines intersected, a super brilliant spot formed and exploded with an energy of ecstasy, like a fountain, igniting the sphere around itself . . .

"Look closely," I heard in my inner mind. "We want you to do this on your planet, too. You can travel these waves of time and light and illuminate the grids of energy around your own planet. It will fill your heart with deep satisfaction because it will allow you to be who you truly are—a being of immense beauty, light, and expansiveness. Simply imagine a network of light lines embracing your planet, and then see this system glow. If it is not totally full of light, ask what the dim areas might need and then see the light of Love fill those points in the grid. See how this Love weaves into all manifested life on earth and how all the creatures are nourished by its deep sense of connection to Love and All-that-Is."

My visionary experience continued, with messages constantly pouring in constantly. "All of you are connected to this web. It feeds information of a higher nature into your own atmosphere and into your Self. By elevating your own self-concept, and seeing that your true body is not only one of flesh and bone but also one of light as great as you can possibly imagine, you increase your own sphere of influence; you become the beauty you imagine."

I could see the gridwork of light flooding ecstasy into the very core of every being in this dimension. It reminded me of tending a garden and weeding if necessary, watching in awe as the flowers of love blossomed in the Souls of all that lived there.

"Your mission, should you accept it, is to increase the frequencies in and on your own world. That truly opens the gates to Heaven wherever you are. Be in awe of the force that sustains all; admire its beauty in everything you see. This in turn will build your connection to the Source, and true miracles will happen."

The images and feelings flooded my inner understanding, and I accepted.

"Now go and let others know," they finished.

With this last message the spiral they had spun around me loosened and I came into my more normal state, noticing that my dolphin friend was right by my side. I had come there to experience a new state of reality and learn about what I as a human could do with the power of intent and awareness through imagery.

I understood that imagery is simply the doorway into dimensions that are otherwise inaccessible to the physical mind. In those other dimensions the past and the future touch hands, and changes along the lines of time manifest in the third-dimensional world.

Gently, my dolphin friend tugged me away, and I wished every being well, deeply thanking them with tears in my eyes. The love, care, and understanding they had for one another and me was so deep. I felt honored.

As we approached planet Earth, we hovered for a while above the globe. From there my dolphin friend showed me the network of light. It was easy to see from the dimension we were in, and I realized how some areas on the planet are more connected to this gridwork than others. "Go now and tell others. Let them know about the water planet that they too can visit. Write everything into your guided-imagery journey, and know that we really do live in multiple dimensions, even though it looks like our bodies only reside in one."

With these last thought-images, my friend bid me farewell and indicated that I could go back to where I had started my journey and he would return to where he started his—at the secret beach.

Within moments I sensed the futon couch underneath me and became aware of the house around me. I felt thrilled by the intricacy with which my ordinary waking life was connected to my imagery life.

I understood that the coincidence of the dream in which I had been zapped by the dolphin's sonar with the guided-imagery journey as described by Lana Miller in her book would initiate my creation of a series of tapes. I also knew that it had not been just a dream. These experiences were of deeper truth, and they hinted at the interconnecting point in life where fact and fiction touch one another and co-create new realities.

Don and I got busy creating a number of guided-imagery journeys and put them on tape. The subjects we chose were: Time Travel, creating or deepening a Spiritual Partnership, Healing, Living Abundantly, Dreamtime Awakening, Healing the Earth and Dolphin Consciousness. As I wrote the text for Quantum Imaging, Mind Journeys, Don wrote the music. Recording and producing were right in line with our abilities and level of experience. We loved to fall into subtle trances as we recorded these journeys, feeling one with each journey we created.

One afternoon, as we were working on the tapes, our Time Traveler called to invite us to a meeting. He wanted us to meet a man by the name of Dr. Rod Newton, who was creating a course on making miracles a daily possibility for everyone.

Before we knew it, we were on our way to a magical meeting.

27

As we drove up to the meeting location, I could feel we were going to enter a new world. The two couples from our first Time Travel seminar at the Rim Institute were also there. All six of us were involved with the SE-5—the instrument of miracles, we all loved inner-dimensional work; and we all had taught subtle dimensional processes.

This meeting turned out to be magical. As we sat brainstorming with Dr. Rod Newton, Moray B. King, and our Time Traveler we discussed the nature of the fabric of life, the nonlinear nature of time, and how we as humans could enter the doorway of Heaven in our daily lives.

Rod had created a course that would allow people to co-create their own version of Heaven on Earth. It was about effectively learning and practicing methods of manifesting our dreams.

These dreams could range from finally getting a door hung in the house to getting a house built, and even to becoming enlightened.

The course was designed to teach effective methods of co-creating in life. As we would discover in the future, participants become brilliant at creating anything from physical experiences to inner experiences. People meet once a week for five weeks for about three hours each time, and they learn the skills that are the foundation for creating anything and realizing one's co-creative influence in life.

At home the participants work with tapes for about ten minutes each morning and evening and also with daily worksheets. As the weeks progress, the skills increasingly involve higher dimensions and allow each person not only to create, but to create in alignment with the purpose of his or her life, his or her "Mission in Life."

Herein lies the most profound difference between this course and simply learning methods of manifesting.

This course is about learning to live in harmony with life and about finding one's higher purpose and how to live it. Within each one of us lies a gift and purpose for our life. When we live in alignment with this higher purpose and the Soul's intent, our focus, imagination, and dreams will be of service to the greater matrix of creation. It is only when we separate ourselves from God, the Source, that our creations become ego-directed. When we are aligned with the Source, God reflects Itself back through the eyes of Its own creation. Our greatest gift to the universe is the awe and joy we feel when we perceive the beauty of God manifest, while at the same time adding the song of our own soul to the symphony and beauty of God.

At times though it isn't easy to see the beauty of life, and often we don't know how to make our first dream come true. How many times have I been a "basket case," or down with PMS, wanting to be filled with light but couldn't get there?

In the months and years that followed, this course became the foundation of manifesting our dreams—from writing books to building houses, from recording CDs to swimming with dolphins. Much of what I was to learn from the dolphins is contained in the course "Living From Vision." It combines elements Don and I had learned from our Time Traveler with exact methods for creating.

I still wonder at the synchronicity of all the learning that came my way in conjunction with exploring the dimensions of the dolphins. The level from which the dolphins work has strong similarities to the practice of imagery.

Rod had finished most of the "Living From Vision" course but still needed a guided-imagery journey for one segment. One of the brainstorming sessions resulted in Don and me writing what became the sixth of our Mind Journeys, "Mission In Life," parts of which would be used in the "Living From Vision" course.

Late one afternoon we presented the journey to the group. The music Don had written previously was out of this world. My gentle voice guided us through the journey. The music happened to fit with every move we made, and I felt as if guided by unseen hands.

"Start by taking a deep breath and relaxing in your chair . . . In your mind's eye, let yourself slowly move up until you float high above the planet . . . moving ever higher, passing the planets of our solar system . . . moving past the Milky Way . . . past other galaxies . . . far beyond any space as we know it . . . until you start entering the dimension of the 'Place of Planning' . . .

"Here you find pure stillness, a place from which you can see all time . . . You start looking over your entire lifetime on earth . . . How has it been? What was it you wanted to learn? What was it you wanted to express? . . . Take your time to allow the answers to come into your understanding, and keep breathing gently . . .

"What was the highest purpose for you this life? . . . How are you doing so far? . . . Is there still something you want to be, do, or experience? . . . As you get a feeling or a sense, honor it, whatever it may be . . .

"Is there a color that could represent that feeling . . . Is there an image, or a symbol? . . . Feel deep inside yourself; sense the wisdom of your soul . . . Are you living in alignment with your highest purpose? What would it feel like if you lived fully in alignment with your purpose and your deeper essence? . . . Let yourself feel the fulfillment of this experience . . . and let this feeling permeate your whole essence, expanding within you the color or image that would best represent living your highest purpose . . . Take all the time you need and want for this experience . . . it is precious . . .

"And when you are ready to start expressing your alignment with your purpose in this life, you can begin by flying back into the world of form, the universe from which you came . . . You start seeing the multicolored galaxies flying by as you head for a familiar galaxy, the Milky Way . . . toward your familiar solar system . . . And then you see the blue planet . . . third one out from the sun . . . planet Earth.

"And as you hover above planet Earth you radiate the feeling of living in alignment with your purpose . . . You send your image, color, or feeling you have for your purpose on a light beam toward your body on planet earth . . . It begins pulsating in your heart . . . and you feel the wisdom you have brought with you from this journey, whether you are consciously aware of it or not . . . "

The gentle music came slowly to an end and everyone started stretching their arms and legs. Inner smiles floated through the room, and I could feel the deepened sense of wisdom. As some participants shared their experiences with the group, a general tenor resounded through each of us. We had come here to learn about Love and to share this Love. It seemed simple.

Inside this lesson of Love, we each carry gifts that we want to share, often hidden in the form of our deeper desires and interests. For me it was interacting with the dreamtime space, discovering the universal laws and God's reflection in them. For others the desire and gift was working with children, healing, or playing music, reflecting the beauty of the spheres for others to hear.

It was wonderful to hear from some of the participants, because I could find myself reflected in many of their observations. What a blessing it was to be able to find so much wisdom in my own heart, which words alone could never describe sufficiently. It was this inner wisdom and strength that Rod Newton was seeking to weave into everyday living with the "Living From Vision" course.

Rod needed feedback on the course, and all of us were to go home and teach the course to our friends in order to see what kind of changes needed to be made. Part of this meeting had been to prepare us to teach. We could have hardly imagined the wonderful impact the course would have on our lives.

We still had a couple of days here at this gathering of "dreamers," and it was a spirited time for us. The night before we left I had an outstanding revelation in a dream.

28

The previous day at our brainstorming session we had discussed why such things as "manifesting" were possible. The zero-point energy, as written about by Moray B. King in his book *Tapping the Zero-Point Energy*, gives clues to the nature of our universe, which allows the imagination to be at the interface between dimensions.

I believe it was these considerations that stirred my desire to understand the deeper working of the universe and that may have given rise to the dream that night. Don and I had gone to bed in a mood of awe and wonder. The clear, starry night sky stretched vastly beyond the limits of our understanding.

"What lies beyond the boundaries of time and space within which lay our physical universe?" we wondered.

As we went to sleep, I held this question in my mind, something I often do when I want to know an answer to which I have no conscious access.

As I was dreaming, I suddenly found myself floating in deep space in the universe at large. An image of a "toroid" floated radiantly before me. It looked like a fountain folded back onto itself, feeding its own roots, much like a doughnut with a very narrow center.

An inner voice told me that this was the image of God, manifest in form. The doughnut was not solid but rather made of lines of energy or light. At its center was a narrow tunnel that marked the transition point between the black hole and the white hole.

Everything that exists is drawn back into the black hole, which retracts everything into itself, into nothingness, and then from this vast vacuum everything is spewed out again through the white hole as a fountain of light.

Such is the way things come into being and dissolve again. It is a continuous cycle of living and dying. Consciousness or awareness manages to survive the transition, except that it is altered by the previous experience.

I saw how the imagination gives form to this mass of light radiating from the white whole. The transformational imagery process we had learned from the Time Traveler tracks any negative event, via feelings and images, to its core. At the core is the point where the black hole becomes the white hole. Here the actual transformation happens. This is possible because every darkness carries a positive potential within it, which is wonderful.

Every black hole is a white hole on the other end, and both are part and parcel of the toroid, the body of creation. Our Time Traveler also used to say that everything, no matter how dark it appears, has a positive intent.

With imagery transformation we are able to move from one dimension to another. Once we can put our finger on something—be it a feeling, an event, or a thing—we can trace its roots back to the black hole from which it is spewed back out into existence through the white hole. Via imagery transformation, we can trace the natural growth pattern and are able to bypass linear time and space and travel *through* the center of the toroid.

As a result of being shown the toroid in my dream I understood the effect of "entropy."

The flow of energy naturally tends to slow down. A train without the push or pull of an engine will slowly come to a halt. Thoughts slow down until they solidify in form and become manifest. If this happens quickly, we call it a miracle; if it happens semi-quickly, we call it coincidence; if it happens slowly, we call it "life."

Entropy is partly a blessing because it gives rise to manifestation, to creation as we know it. And yet it is also what makes life difficult, because we have to push constantly against this force. Dust accumulates if we don't clean up. This cleaning up mechanism is consciousness in action and it is called the "syntropic" force. It comes in many shapes, forms, and levels of expression, but fundamentally it is a force that stimulates life into expansion.

Every morning when we wake up, we need to do some "consciousness house cleaning." By virtue of our focus, we create the molds or forms into which the essence of the universe flows. *Unless we polish these molds into ever-expanding forms of beauty, unless we clean our inner house of consciousness, the force of entropy will compost our creations and us with it.* Our task is to become increasingly more all-encompassing in our awareness, to become an ever more radiant mirror for God. In this balanced dance we find entropy and syntropy, the two playmates of God's creation. The result is increased awareness.

The higher our vantage point within creation the more we are able to embrace that which lies "below." What previously seemed divided into negative and positive becomes part and parcel of the checkerboard of Life. The light and dark parcels belong to the same game.

The white holes and the black holes constitute what scientists call the "quantum foam." This quantum foam is organized in the shape of a toroid, which is often symbolically represented by an infinity sign, the figure eight on its side.

What understanding my dream stimulated! It was wilder than I could have asked for, and I was filled with deep respect for the "imagery work." How simple it looks from the outside. Children can learn it, yet it *is* the secret key many people wish to find.

The next morning after telling Don about my dream, I shared it and my new understanding with our group. Heads nodded enthusiastically. We started to get excited about the implications, and we realized it is *what* we believe possible that determines our so-called limits. In truth, life is an ever-expanding sea of new limits and boundaries. In our group of free thinkers, we created a field of our next human potential within ourselves.

In our culture too much emphasis has been put on cognitive thinking, which only allows a very linear unfolding of time. It is this cognitive thinking that keeps us cut off from much deeper and richer interaction with Life.

Moray likened the solely rational way of thinking, so exalted by science, to seeing Life as a "Flatlander" would see it. As we all discussed a newer model of the universe, Moray demonstrated his idea of the Flatlander.

He had us cut two holes in a sheet of paper and hold the paper flat, about one to two inches above the tabletop. Next he had us insert one finger into each hole and pretend we lived in Flatland where we could only see between the tabletop and the sheet of paper. When we described what we saw, we all started laughing. Each description was funnier than the previous one. "Two round fleshy columns floating down, or two similar but different looking sausages appearing out of the sky" . . . and on and on. No one was able to see that these two fingers belonged to one hand, because in Flatland we could only accept the information that appeared between the tabletop and the sheet of paper. In truth, the two fleshy columns were both connected to a single hand, and it is the third dimensional view that the Flatlander cannot see.

We humans tend to be very similar to Flatlanders. Most of our Western schooling has discredited, even ridiculed, any perception from other dimensions beyond the known physical world. When we think of someone and then they call us on the phone, we tend to write it off as "coincidence." In reality, we have connected in another dimension and are experiencing communication faster than the speed of light. The telephone call is the result of an interaction that happened in another dimension.

When we open to the idea that we exist within many dimensions and allow for the kinds of choices that are influenced by realities beyond our logical mind, then we can start recognizing the forces at work in our life and cooperate with them. Creating a magical life grows out of allowing oneself to interact consciously with a multidimensional reality.

We left the group that afternoon thrilled by the profound implications of this imagery work.

29

The next two months proved to be more than I had hoped for. Don and I set out to teach the course "Living From Vision." We gathered with a number of our friends and offered the course at cost. We met one evening each week and practiced the new skills. We started dreaming and expressing our hopes, and we learned to identify what we loved and valued. Through feelings and images we ventured in our imagination into the potential of our purpose.

Each day we practiced speaking the language of metaphors, the language of the subconscious mind, and modeled ourselves after our inner advisors, the beings who helped us manifest our dreams. If ever I had a doubt that imaginary beings could accomplish actual work, it was put completely to rest during this time. It was as though we had hired little fairies to help us.

We learned about the power of *creating from the end.* As if to emphasize the potential power of this exercise, I "coincidentally" ran into a scientist-researcher at a gemstone exhibit in Seattle shortly after we had started practicing this method. As we gazed at a billion-year old crystal, he told me about a "radically" new way of figuring out a problem.

He explained the process to me thus. "To discover the answer to a question or to find out how to resolve a problem successfully, you start at the end. Through the use of your imagination, you put yourself at the finale, the place where the problem has been figured out, and then look to see what the previous step was that led to the successful result. You continue to do this, going backward in time until you arrive at the present moment when you formulated the question."

What a confirmation! I had just been studying this method with our practice group and loved the results. It felt as if the ancient knowledge within this age old gemstone had prompted this sharing. Maybe there was truth in the saying that the beginning lies in the end and the end lies in the beginning.

The scientist-researcher sadly admitted that this type of knowledge, though practiced by a few leading-edge scientists, would probably take decades to make its way into the everyday knowledge of the masses—if it ever did.

We applied this method to our personal lives in the "Living From Vision" course. For example, we pretended to see a movie of our life as it would be if we had successfully lived it to the end. When I wrote my own eulogy, I wrote to my heart's content. I had become a successful author, teacher, and lecturer, sharing from my heart methods that helped humanity evolve on its path to Oneness with the Source and become conscious co-creators of Heaven on Earth. It felt good to let myself become all that I could dream of.

Every morning and evening we listened to tapes that reinforced the new habits. It felt wonderful to end each day by clearing our minds of leftover concerns and unfinished business. Our goals and dreams started pouring in.

For one of his goals during the "Living From Vision"

course, Don decided to write a book about the SE-5. In his imagery he included the image of selling the book at an upcoming conference where we were scheduled to speak. He used the metaphoric image his subconscious mind had given him for the completed project, which was the image of a flying eagle. When he was actually able to finish the book, get it printed and have it ready to sell at the conference, both of us were floored. It all had happened in the record time of about five weeks!

In one of the subsequent "Living From Vision" courses Don and I taught, I decided that the basement of our house needed to be finished. We had guests coming to stay with us in our newly built geodesic dome, and we needed some private space for them. Don tried to dissuade me, knowing how much effort it would take and thinking that it would only be with extraordinary luck that we could get some of it done in five weeks. But to no avail. I insisted that I wanted a guest bedroom, and we only had one week left before our guests arrived. My metaphorical image was of balloons pinned to the wall. The balloons represented the completion of the project and the party I would throw at that time.

The fifteen-hundred-square foot basement was stacked with "basement garbage." Even the drywall taper, whom I called for an estimate shook his head in disbelief. "Well," I thought, "we can always try." Don agreed and we got started. I still cannot comprehend how it all got done, since I knew the enormous amount of work we had put into building the upper part of the house. But lo and behold, in *seven days* we had the drywall finished in all the rooms. The walls were taped, mudded, and painted, and the carpet was laid and the doors hung. Needless to say we threw the party at the end of our guests' stay.

The man in the couple visiting, Eldon Byrd, had been a friend of Uri Geller, who is famous for metal bending and other anomalous abilities. Eldon had learned how to do metal bending, and at our party he volunteered to teach all of us too. We rushed to buy all the silverware from the thrift stores in the vicinity of our island and got ready.

Everyone at the party wanted to learn how to bend metal, even the most staunch critic in the group. We each got several forks and spoons with which to practice. Eldon guided us into a relaxed state. We slowly let go by breathing deeply, sensing the weight of our bodies on our chairs, as we were guided to visualize his images. In a calm voice he instructed us.

"Imagine feeling the palms of your hands getting warmer and warmer, with energy coming from your heart, traveling through your arms, and filling your hands . . . Imagine a sun above your head, and let the warmth and strength of the sun radiate through your arms and out your hands, increasing in brightness and intensity . . ."

At the culmination of this imagery exercise Eldon instructed us to shout "Bend! Bend! Bend!" and I saw the unbelievable before my very own eyes. Forks and spoons started curling up in everyone's hands. Metal started looking more like butter, and we all danced and laughed and shouted. It was quite overwhelming to see such breaking of physical laws as we know them taking place in plain view.

Collectively we had allowed ourselves to be different.

Together we had created a safe haven in which to be different, and yet still be the same. This collective boundary is an envelope that enfolds us into a unit of wholeness. At the same time, it is also a major source of limitation on our personal growth. Our deep-seated desire and survival need is to belong, to be the same as others around us. If we didn't mimic everything in our social surroundings, we would not speak the same language, nor use the same subtle body language and facial expressions.

In simple terms, we would not understand one another. We need to honor this social force. On the one hand it holds us in check and keeps us from becoming too different from those around us, which we may experience as limiting. On the other hand, it provides safety and assures our emotional and physical survival.

Eldon's stories, however, which he told us before his guided-imagery session, convinced us. Others, he had said, some of them very reputable people, had done the metal bending before us. Our subconscious must then have reasoned that it was okay for all of us. Only one person said he couldn't do it. This man had been the most critical, most questioning. He was disappointed and yet felt justified. The sad part was that his critical orientation had limited his imagery capacities, although part of him had wanted to change. Just as he was getting ready to leave and was saying goodbye to us, still fiddling with his fork he suddenly shouted "I did it, I did it!" At last he had let go, and in that moment of letting go there was the power to create change.

This learning *how to let go* is part of the "Living From Vision" course. Letting go creates the "zero-point" at which the force of creation gains entry into our dimension. It's funny how things happen just at the point when we don't care any longer. Letting go is the secret.

Don and I loved the "Living From Vision" course. Not only were we manifesting objective realities, such as the book on the SE-5 and the guest bedroom, we also applied the same processes to our inner dimensions. We focused on our relationship, our love life, our lucid dreams, and states of bliss and ecstasy.

We were stunned. Our life flowed more flawlessly than it ever had before, and a deep sense of self-appreciation settled in. We were getting the results we wanted and we accomplished the goals on which we focused. The results were so convincing that I decided to translate the course into German and to start training teachers in Germany. This helped fulfill my soul's desire to give something back to the culture in which I had grown up.

We also wanted to teach the English version more extensively, but there was one slight problem: I did not like the female voice that Rod had chosen for the tapes. Don and other seminar participants felt the same way. Her pitch was too high for my taste, and I could not relax with it. After much deliberation we decided to tell Rod that the course was excellent but the female voice was not very pleasing. He agreed, as it wasn't the first time he had heard this comment, and he considered redoing the tapes.

As Christmas came around and I had finished the translation of the material into my native language, I was ready to record the German version of the "Living From Vision" tapes. Rod sat in on the recording and listened to what sounded like babble as he did not understand German. He did like the sound of my voice, however, and in an inspired moment decided to dub my voice over the previous female voice on his English tapes. It was Christmas Eve, and there we sat in the studio dubbing my voice over the previous one. In Germany, my family and I would have been gathering around the Christmas tree on this evening to sing the old, holy German Christmas songs about angels and miracles.

Maybe the angels appreciated the effort we were making and blessed the tapes; they do seem to have magic in them.

30

Christmas came and went and the new year brought more creative projects. Luckily, here in the Northwest spring is long and starts very early. In February the first leaves sprouted on the bushes, promising longer days of sun, and the air took on a smell of excitement.

The "Living From Vision" course was here to stay. In our early spring class Don and I chose the image of swimming with dolphins to represent our next goal. We needed to create enough money to pay for our taxes, buy airline tickets, and have spending money while in Hawaii. We also needed to create the emotional and internal space inside of us to allow dolphins into our presence.

Halfway through the course we "miraculously" had enough money to pay our income taxes. And by the end of the course we had the additional money needed for our trip to Hawaii. It was also during this course that Don decided he wanted to become proficient at drawing. His stick figures made him feel rather childish and he needed to improve his art ability.

In retrospect, I realize how his desire fit into the grander scheme of things, although at the time I did not see any need for it. Eventually Don would design ads for our national advertising campaign and create covers for our CDs and books. His artistic abilities needed to be more developed. Maybe it was the wise guidance of his inner "higher" self that prompted him to feel the urge to draw. Whatever the reasons, he added drawing to his goals.

It just so happened that our Time Traveler had to cancel a week-long seminar with us. We had planned to take a group of people back through time to heal old patterns and wounds laying hidden in their past lives and/or past lineage. For this event we had booked space at a Buddhist retreat center and had already paid an advance to secure our reservation. Because of our commitment we needed to fulfill our obligation, so Don and I stayed at the center for five days in compensation for the cancellation. We welcomed this "time out." As we arrived in the misty mountains of southern Washington, we took a deep breath. The soothing energy of the pine trees enveloped us, and the simple living environment of rustic cabins made us feel relaxed and at peace immediately. Vegetarian meals served communally with the center's residents and plenty of time to meditate gave us a chance to slow down. Many small things started feeling grand and important again.

I remember taking a walk one evening up a small hill where the light of the fading sun gave the clouds delicious hues of pink. A small lake stretched before us, the grass still wet from a misty rain earlier in the afternoon and the birds had begun their evening songs. A tall, dark pine tree stood to our left, and the rising fog from the evening's mist shrouded the lake in front of us. A pink cloud above the lake had formed into an oval-shaped flat disc and made me feel as if we were floating in a higher dimension.

Suddenly I realized that this image was like the metaphoric image I had created in the "Living From Vision" course to represent traveling in inner dimensions in order to be in touch with my inner worlds. By "coincidence" we had had to take this "time out" trip, since we were responsible for part of the payment due to the cancellation. Here I was, after days of leisure time, feeling like my inner vision was receiving the amount of rest it had wanted. Not only did I have this experience, but I also got to see my metaphor "live" in front of me. "What you focus on is what you get," our Time Traveler had always said. How true!

This course was miraculous! As part of Don's desire to draw we brought with us Betty Edwards's book *Drawing on the Right Side of Your Brain*, and he followed the instructions step by step. His first drawing was to serve as a yardstick, and reflected his level of ability at that time. He drew a portrait of me. A round circle represented my head; two round circles stood in for my eyes; and long lines around the head reflected my hair. It didn't look much like me, but it was a good beginning!

The surprise came two days later when he turned from drawing stick figures to full portraits. At the end of our stay, as he drew the last portrait of me, I could hardly believe my eyes. Here I was on a sheet of paper, shades of light playing over my face and reflecting my immersion in deep thought. All the proportions were so amazingly true to my face, the shades of dark and light giving it the plasticity of real life. I could hardly fathom that this had been drawn by Don, who had indeed become an artist. My progress had equaled Don's, except that I started out being fairly good at drawing already. It had been my teenage hobby. And as good as he became, I also improved that much in my own development as an artist. We were stunned by our progress.

Betty Edwards tells you at the beginning of her book that this miraculous transformation will happen if you follow her outline step by step. On the first pages she shows portraits created by students both *before* and *after* they have completed her class. We thought she probably had picked the best examples and that some people would, of course, have such dramatic results. But us?

Betty Edwards discovered that if we learn to engage the right side of our brain, we drastically improve our abilities. It reminded me of Dr. Rod Newton's "Living From Vision" course. Rod Newton created this course to help people access, step by step, the deeper resources of the right side of the brain and apply them to daily living. Students learn how to speak to the right side of the brain and give it metaphorical images to create virtually anything they want.

The results from Rod's course are as amazing as the "before and after" pictures in Betty Edwards's book. Why are such things not yet taught in our schools? Why is there so much focus on the linear, sequential mind? Why didn't we learn these skills from our ancestors? American Indians learned to talk to stones and trees, and the land spoke with wisdom to their hearts. It is through this way of listening that we can hope to live in cooperation with life.

The thoughts of American Indians reminded us of a woman who had attended one of our seminars some time ago. We had co-taught the seminar with our Time Traveler and stayed in touch with the participants.

Weeks after the seminar she told us the following story. She had been dating a real-estate developer who had been desperately trying to sell a piece of land in Utah for the last two years. She told him about the inner-dimensional implications of imagery work, and he was interested to see what she could do with the land.

In her mind she went to her Place of Peace and called

upon the presence of her inner luminous Self. She extended her feeling to the piece of land as though it were a living being with a voice and wishes of its own. In her imagination she sent questions to the land, and it told her that it felt discredited, mistreated and dishonored by being treated like an object. The land had not been listened to for a long time and had managed to hold up the realtors and their projects. Sensing the soul of the land, she asked what it needed in order to feel honored and if it agreed with the plan to create a settlement around a small artificial lake.

The land's soul sent her the message that it wanted to be acknowledged for the higher purposes and possibilities still hidden in its essence. It wanted to be honored in a ceremony that addressed the many spirit beings who lived there and have her ask for their cooperation and assistance in creating a higher space for people to live in.

The land had a voice and needed its feelings honored. These concepts are totally foreign to most Western minds, but this woman had seen results in her private practice of the imagery process. Subsequently, she did the ceremony on the land and communicated in her imagination with the other spirits there. She asked for their permission and their assistance, all the while honoring them, perhaps for the first time since white people had settled in the area. The land and its spirit beings felt honored and were willing to help in the bigger plan.

Although her boyfriend had been a "Facts and Figures" person, he could not ignore the "coincidence" when the land sold immediately, and he signed up for the next seminar.

Wisdom of the Dolphins

With this in mind, one day I decided to see if I could do something about the dolphins' plight. At the time there was news about fishermen slaughtering dolphins in an attempt to catch ever greater amounts of tuna. I had already boycotted tuna, yet I sensed that I might be able to enter the inner dimensions in order to help the dolphins.

31

I had held in my heart the desire to somehow help dolphins ever since our Time Traveler had told us about the transformation of the gaseous orange cloud into "peace games." Finally, one afternoon I felt the time was right. It was a warm and definite inner nudge that prompted me to sit down on our balcony overlooking the Puget Sound.

Big gray whales had been swimming in our bay this year, which was a rare occurrence, and I felt honored by their presence. Early that morning we had heard the blow of the whales as they exhaled through the big blowhole on top of their heads. Water sprayed up like a fountain, and the sound was loud enough to stir us out of our sleep.

I started pondering the world of cetaceans. Whales and dolphins are members of the same family, with dolphins being termed "small whales." They are air-breathing mammals, who birth their young like humans, breast-feeding and attending to the little ones until they have learned the basics of their language and social interaction skills and can catch their own food.

Their language abilities become increasingly more complex as they grow older and wiser. John Lilly graphed the vocalizations of dolphins and discovered a drastic increase in complexity as they matured. And just like humans, some adults have greater capacities than others. This finding confirmed the feelings I had from my telepathic contact with them. It felt as if some dolphins have more "say" and leadership qualities, as well as greater wisdom, than others. Essentially we are dealing with evolved beings, just like ourselves. Along with whales, dolphins are the most intelligent beings in the ocean, and I personally feel they are the most evolved conscious beings on the planet. They have had highly evolved brains for millions of years, whereas humans have undergone less than one hundred thousand years of meaningful evolution and have only had an evolved brain for less than forty thousand years.

The cetacean family of dolphins and whales originally lived on the land and then retreated to the seas; they still carry vestiges of finger bones in their pectoral fins. We humans use our fingers for manipulating physical objects, while the dolphins and whales do not have this capacity. What do they use their greater brain capacity for? It appears that their social abilities and the intricacies of social interaction as well as their inter-dimensional communications are far more developed than in humans.

The fact that whales have a global communication network and have had it for millions of years *without* the use of technology should make us think. Humans have only recently developed that ability and only with the help of advanced technology.

At this point in time, humans are threatening to disrupt the ecosphere in order to afford such communication abilities. We are threatening the oceans by sending low-frequency sounds through the waters in order to determine if we are experiencing global warming, and if so, how much. This does not speak favorably about human intelligence.

What seems low-level to us could significantly disturb the communications whales have developed over millions of years, and the act of broadcasting these frequencies could be likened to aliens coming to Earth and sending disruptive microwave frequencies to incapacitate our satellite communication system. Many humans do not honor their great cousins in the water. Technological profits seem to be more important.

At the time of my pondering, dolphins were, and unfortunately still are being knowingly slaughtered in the attempt to catch more and more fish. Schools of tuna swim for some unknown reason underneath pods of dolphins in the open sea. Fishermen use the easily sighted fins of dolphins as a telltale sign that lots of tuna are nearby. As the fishermen set their nets to catch the fish, they also catch the dolphins.

I sat on our balcony that afternoon attempting to create some healing in the ethers and in the dreamscape of my universe, hoping to somehow help the dolphins survive.

I slowly closed my eyes, and started to focus on the issue. I took a deep breath and asked the dolphins and my inner guides to help me in my imagery and let only that come to pass that was of the highest benefit to all beings concerned.

Soon I was floating in my inner vision high above the clouds, though I was not really traveling. I looked at the entire planet. How I loved this planet. It looked like a sparkling jewel to me in the midst of space. Mentally I asked where the major companies were located that were participating in the massive slaughter of dolphins in tuna nets. Three places emerged as if pointed out on a map. With an inner knowing I saw one company located on the California Coast, another one by the Texas gulf coast, and one in Japan. To see this field of information I utilized the same sense as when I talk to my inner images. I checked each one of them for the possibility of working successfully and easily with them. Japan's energy seemed hardened at the time, and the session would have gone beyond my means, so I looked at the remaining two companies. The company in California seemed to promise the easiest transformation, so I honed in on it. In my mind I searched for the "leadership" energy. Searching for this "head" energy was similar to what I did the evening I communicated with the "leader" of the dolphin pod before we met at 8:45 A.M. at the secret beach.

The leader energy image of this tuna company looked like a spiking triangle, and it let me know that it was willing to communicate. I "showed" myself, (my energy body, that is), and I sent my intention, "I come in peace." I honored this company's entity as fully as if it were a conscious being, which for all practical purposes it was, and I sent pictures of the dolphin slaughtering and the tuna fishing with the question "Why?"

Quickly I received the answer that this was a responsible company interested in providing food for humans and supporting all the people who worked for it, provided parents the ability to care for their families, and killing dolphins was part and parcel of the fishing business. I acknowledged the purpose of this company and saw the dilemma they were in. I honored the intent of providing for a community of humans.

In a flash I sent back the image and message of the many people who were disgusted with the atrocious killing of dolphins. I also sent an image of how these people would be demonstrating their upset by ceasing to buy tuna, which would defeat the purpose of the company.

"Could there be another more harmonious way of

providing food for humans and satisfying the company's responsibilities to its employees and their families that would let the dolphins live, thereby creating a better public image and a possible increase, instead of decrease, in sales?" I mentally asked.

The answer came back with a beautiful light, "Yes! There are other options that could protect the dolphins!" The image I saw was one of light-filled understanding, represented by a mountain peak with a harmonious field of flowers casting their fragrances and colors over the slopes.

I followed the same process that I used in all my personal transformations, allowing the old image to become absorbed into the new image; only this time it was the image of an entity, a company.

I sincerely thanked this entity for its cooperation. After it had transformed itself, it became part of the manifested matrix of life, letting the fountain of life-giving energy touch the earth.

As the imagery process completed, I opened my eyes and stretched my body. I was moved by the depth of the communication and had the feeling that something global had really transpired. I anchored myself back into reality by looking at the spring flowers all around me and quickly let go of all questions like: "Did it really happen? Will it work?" I had done my part like others before me, and if this change was in harmony with the universe, and it wanted it to work, it would. This process felt so organic.

Everything in life wants to grow and evolve, and in the process the old forms are shed and become new ones. The black hole turns into the white hole, and a new reality blossoms.

I pondered some of the spiritual beliefs in which the ultimate state is the "no state," the void or the detachment from life. Making changes in the matrix of life makes no sense from that perspective. Yet, as I see it, there is no way to stop the process of life unfolding, since all life stems from one seed, which one may call God, and *It* desires to be. If *It* had desired to be undone, life would already have annihilated itself. Had that been possible it would have already happened and manifestation would no longer be.

Yet life provides a playground in which it can learn to love and become all that it is capable of becoming. In the process of life, the inborn mechanism for evolution and growth expresses itself everywhere, and it is the secret of why this imagery work is so effective, at least in one's personal life.

But could this imagery work effectively on a global scale? And if so, to what degree? Was it a reliable process? How would one ever know?

32

Soon I was to find out some answers to these questions. In late Spring, a couple of months after the "Living From Vision" course, we prepared to host another seminar with our Time Traveler. Maybe a part of us knew that the time with him was running out and we would soon find ourselves on our own, navigating through time and space, discovering more and more of the true fabric from which life is created. But for now we still had him with us.

Meanwhile we had met a woman named Dr. Bobbie Barnes, who also had learned the imagery process from the Time Traveler. She had written her Ph.D. thesis on utilizing the imagery processes with at-risk students in a California school district. During two months of summer vacation, she was able to raise the students' scholastic standing, measurably increase their self-esteem, and fill them with so much enthusiasm that they brought more of their friends into this program. Some of these children had lived on the streets, handled guns, used drugs, etc. When they learned to meet their own "Full Potential Self," they changed and started to turn their lives around. Bobbie Barnes's work deeply moved and inspired me.

One of the participants in our seminar was such a teenage high school dropout when I first met him. He had chosen to drive a truck and make money instead of finishing school. His father, a supervisor at a large company in Seattle, had participated in the first seminar and brought his wife and son to the next one. His wife suffered from insomnia, always kept the curtains drawn in her house during the daytime and had been preparing to die. She was dangerously depressed. The images she carried in her subconscious looked so dark, even from across the room, that I asked Don if he could assist her in her processes.

Her images were full of gloom. Blood-dripping dark clouds took all her life's energy. Yet despite the intense darkness those internal images portrayed, she managed to talk to these monsters, understand their deeper purpose, love them, and let them become the powerful allies she had always wanted.

By the second seminar her life force had become strong again, and with the clearing of her own past during the Re-Creation Seminar she turned her life completely around. Up went the curtains in the house of her life. The dark clouds transformed into allies who wanted to assist her in the fulfillment of her life's purpose. Her desire was to help Russian mythology survive. According to her information Russian myths were no longer taught in Russian schools. Communism had wiped out any sense of the old roots.

Out of the blue, shortly after the significant changes she had made during the seminar, Russian dignitaries came to her house for a dinner party. In turn they invited her to Russia, and arranged for a visa. Six months later, after having learned some Russian, this mom traveled on her own to Russia, never before in her life having traveled without her husband. Once she arrived in Russia everything fell into place, and various university professors helped her accomplish her goal.

During this particular seminar in late spring all three members of her family were present. The son had started working on his GED after the last seminar so that he could prepare to enter college.

The spring blossoms had filled the air with sweet fragrances and the cherries were in full bloom. As I sat in front of this young man during the seminar, guiding him through his imagery, I was filled with awe and love for his being. Not long ago he had had such a bad energy field around him, with greasy hair and an unpleasant smell that discouraged anyone from working with him. As an assistant, our Time Traveler had volunteered me, and I "had" to work with him. Sometimes we are forced into our luck.

Here I sat, watching him radiate more and more beauty as his images matured. He was quite heavyset and as he opened his eyes deep wisdom shone forth from his soul. I said to him, "You remind me of a whale, Andrew." His big body size and his wise eyes moved me.

"I feel like one," he answered with a sense of being seen for who he was. We understood in that still moment of time that in truth we are each an amazing jewel in the universe.

Our conversation drifted onto whales and dolphins and suddenly he said, "Did you read the news today?! A tuna company just announced that they are not going to kill dolphins anymore and instead have shifted to a different form of fishing."

I was dazed. "Is it a company located somewhere in California?" I quickly asked.

"Yes, I believe so," he answered thoughtfully, puzzled

about the tears in my eyes. I told him about my imagery session a while back, and we both looked at each other for a long time, starting to drift into the heightened space of understanding the matrix of life.

As I looked into his eyes I saw time and space stretched out before me as a fabric made of intersecting light lines. I saw how our awareness was animating this matrix of light. If we could rise sufficiently high in our vantage point and carry within us enough love to understand and embrace that which lay "below" us, we could be at any place in any universe we chose to be.

I saw his many faces as I stared into his open eyes: his Egyptian leanings, the teacher he was; the healer he was, and the wisdom he allowed to shine forth. A year later I would find him again in Germany, though now in another body called Andreas. Through many seminars we saw him lose his whale costume, and become empowered, as a teacher and a healer.

People or souls had been shape-shifting more and more often in my life. People came to visit me through other people's bodies, or I felt a continuation of one kind of relationship with a human in a different body. Maybe I projected my expectations—certainly psychology would explain my experiences that way—but I became more and more convinced that we, as Soul, move through space and time a lot more fluidly than our culture teaches us is possible.

Sometimes friends called me up from far-away places and told me of a chance encounter they had that day with a person who looked *just like me*, gave hugs *just like me,* and talked of dolphins *just like me*. They felt that I was visiting them. The difficult part was not to confuse the person who seemed to be lending his or her "services," with my soul essence.

Sometimes I noticed that people even shape-shifted right before eyes. One moment they looked like one person; the next they looked identical to a close friend of mine, speaking like he or she would and relating with me as if they were this other friend. I had to hold myself back sometimes not to be too friendly, or else I might have given them the wrong impression.

Once I flew to a seminar that a close friend had wanted to attend with me. Due to family complications he was unable to come along. At the airport Don was seeing me off and pointed out a person who was such a "look-alike" to my friend that we had to take a second look. What a surprise it was to find this particular man walking down the isle and take a seat right next to me! We started talking and soon were discussing theories of time shifts and other new scientific viewpoints. I could not help but notice how much this man started sounding like my friend, on a flight which my friend had intended to take but didn't.

The more we talked, the more I was moved. Soon he was quiet, simply looked me in the eyes, and I could not help but see the worlds I had shared with my friend in years before.

Social necessities had prevented us from seeing one another, but here I was seeing him nevertheless. My heart pounded, and inside I started to shake. Tears came to my eyes, and I turned my head away, pretending to look out the window. My neighbor started inquiring if I was all right, and I thought it might not be prudent to tell him of my observation. But I did anyway. I told him about my friend, about how I had perceived his presence shifting into our communication and what this meant to me.

The man was not surprised. Although he came from a traditional scientific background, he had noticed the change in himself and it didn't scare him. Instead he started tuning in more and became a willing bridge for my friend's soul and me. He told me of how "he," now as my friend, felt deep down inside, why it was that "he," as my friend, was making certain choices, and his eyes told me the rest. Sometimes I leaned over to see if my friend wasn't just playing a trick on me, having put on big, black-framed reading glasses in order to bluff me.

No, he hadn't. At the end of the flight at Dulles International Airport in Washington, D.C., this gentleman went out of his way to help me find the connecting flight and told me that he did not want my phone number. Nor did I want his. We knew he had been a surrogate, a bridge, and he had allowed himself to be conscious of it. He was deeply grateful for the experience in his otherwise rather normal life.

Maybe it was good that my friend chose not to come along. Our human and social boundaries are real, and breaking them only causes hardship. In the end we often revert back to what feels safe, even if it is less filled with light. However, our souls had found a way to bridge for a moment the separation in time and space, enough so that I was able to see the truth in our hearts.

The world around Don and I had been shifting, and we

started feeling that the solidly real structure of the three-dimensional world was not necessarily what our culture had taught us to believe it was. The veil was lifting, and in the blink of an eye we could choose to wake up in another world. The way we moved into new dimensions was by shifting imagery in our minds and realizing that the outer life was a reflection of our inner picture show. It was only our individual belief system that determined how far we could jump.

33

Let's return for a moment to the time when Don and I finished the last "Living From Vision" course, during which we had set our goals of paying taxes and swimming with dolphins again. We managed to create enough funds to do both, and every participant in our class had created his or her own miracles. Some had goals of increasing their spiritual awareness; others wanted to find a life partner, remodel a house, or do their life's work. I was touched by the fact that everyone had improved his or her life dramatically. The fact that many had some previous knowledge of the skills taught in the "Living From Vision" course seemed only to add to the results. We loved to repeat the class ourselves. No matter how many times Don and I taught this course, we wanted to teach it again for all the amazing results we were able to create.

Our trip to Hawaii was now only a few days away. We were going to explore Maui this time, and we planned to stay with Linda and her partner at the bed and breakfast they owned. We had first met them at the health food store in Kauai during our last trip, and the promise of the Zodiac ride in order to find dolphins had stayed in our minds. We were eager and ready to leave for Hawaii.

In the last few months I had been "talking" to the whales in the bay in front of our house and let them know that we would be going to visit their dolphin cousins in Hawaii. I was hoping they would hear me and send a long-distance message to their cousins off Maui. The last four days before leaving, however, we hadn't seen any whales. A pod of gray whales had come from California in early spring and dropped off the old and very young in the bays of Puget Sound by Seattle to rest and feed while the rest of the pod went up north to the waters of Alaska.

Suddenly, just as we got ready to get into our car to go to the airport, we heard the loud sound of the unmistakable whoosh. The spray of the whale's breath was still hanging in midair as I turned to look for it. Had he or she come to say good-bye, I wondered? Did whales understand our thoughts? I felt it was a good sign and we headed off to the airport.

As luck would have it the flight was overbooked, and one of the airline agents asked for volunteers to take a later flight in exchange for a $250 flight coupon. Don and I jumped at the chance and volunteered. It did not make any difference to us since we would arrive in Maui only a few hours later.

Finally, the rescheduled flight to Honolulu was ready to depart. We were excited and filled with anticipation. Our thoughts buzzed around swimming with dolphins. This time we had imaged *being with* dolphins, swimming with them, and we *felt* the *fulfilled feelings* instead of visualizing the desired result as a carrot in front of us.

We had to go through Honolulu International airport, and while waiting at the gate I got a flash of Go Pal Das, my blue-eyed, blond haired inner guide. He shone brightly, hovering in midair, and looked lovingly upon me. "You are going to meet me again in form, but this time please make sure you don't confuse me with the body of the person through whom I will visit you," he whispered. "You have called me." I shook at the thought of it. Indeed I had sent a rather urgent message to him.

I missed him and wanted confirmation that my imaginings were not solely a product of my own fantasy. Yet meeting him the last time, when his love shone through the eyes of Paul on Kauai had nearly cost me my mind, although I had tried not to show it. Don had kindly helped me set my head straight, and I was not sure that I wanted to expose myself again to such a multiple-reality challenge. With most normal mortals the visits from beyond the boundaries of time and space seemed manageable, but with him it was different; he had a magnetism to which my soul was attracted that was beyond linear understanding.

After a short island hop we landed safely on Maui. As we walked down the isle toward baggage claim, I started hearing the soft sound of a conch shell. The sound came mysteriously from high above, and I thought I was hearing faint rumbles of drums.

Hawaiian music filled the air, and from a reality deeper than the physical I heard an invitation spoken. Almost as if the island spirit of the volcanoes that had built the Hawaiian islands were speaking to us, I heard a voice welcoming us to the islands and telling us that someday they were going to be our home. The island spirit wanted us to stay. I was awed and didn't know what to make of it. By the time we got to the car rental booth, the sun was almost setting and we headed south to Kihei.

As we entered "Hale Hana," our friend's bed and breakfast, we were greeted by the most luminous eyes sparkling with love and inner joy. Linda helped us settle into our comfortable room. The covered porch outside was the outdoor living room, and fuchsia-colored bougainvilleas arched over the walkways.

Early the next morning, while Don was still sleeping, I sat outside on the porch to meditate. I felt deep gratitude for the early morning songs of the doves and other Hawaiian birds that transported me immediately into a sense of tropical paradise. Soon I was drifting into higher and higher spaces and saw the face of Go Pal Das again. My love for him had soared ever since I had met him in one of my dreams.

In my dream he had been a teacher in a monastery where I was a teacher in training. At a crucial moment he had looked deeply into my eyes and radiated profound love into my heart, the likes of which I have never experienced in my physical life. He saw my true essence and I saw his. We became indebted to one another forever and were to assist in each other's evolution—although at present it looked like he was mostly helping me.

Faintly I heard footsteps passing nearby, which then receded toward the balcony. Soon the footsteps returned and settled right in front of me. "Should I continue to meditate, or should I have a look?" I wondered. I decided to gently open my eyes to acknowledge the other person's presence and see if it was Don who had come to be with me. As soon as I lifted my eyelids I shut them again tightly. Had I not been sitting, I probably would have fallen down. It couldn't be! A man with blue eyes and blond shoulder-length hair was sitting in front of me. Go Pal Das hadn't been kidding. Unbelievable! If this was true I was going to become a believer in all my fantasies.

"Hi!" I said, trying to sound normal. "My name is Ilona."

"Hi, nice to meet you; my name is Carl," he replied in a friendly voice, grinning from ear to ear.

"Oh brother," I thought, "if this isn't Go Pal Das I better make sure he doesn't think I am some kind of an available Maui vacationer." Quickly I clued him in. "My partner Don and I are here for a couple of weeks; we're hoping to meet dolphins."

He got the message and yet kept looking at me with his deep blue eyes. Without a moment's notice, we turned our attention to subtler realms. We lifted in a spiral of light, spinning upward, and were transported into the high heavens of union in our souls. "How did he know?" I wondered, and soon I was lost in the beauty of the moment. Love was all that counted in these dimensions, and the precious moments of Oneness in Spirit filled every fiber of my soul. "There is nothing wrong with seeing into the Source of each other," I told myself. In truth there is only magnificence in each and every soul, if we just open our hearts enough to let the light of God shine through.

In the background I heard Don stirring in the room adjacent to the porch, and soon he walked out to see me sitting here with the stranger. I gave him a quick look of "I don't know how on earth this semblance of Go Pal Das manifested here," and Don give me a quick smirk back. We must have been quite a sight. Our cultural boundaries do not include meeting beings from other dimensions, let alone meeting soul to soul in another time. Luckily, Carl had the sense to make space for Don and me and instantaneously seemed to give "right of way" to Don. How subtly we negotiate territories!

"So you want to see dolphins," he started. "I think you'll need to go out on a boat, maybe even over to the island of Lanai, since we don't have a reliable bay for dolphins here on Maui. They do come in sometimes, but it is hit and miss. I have some friends who go out on a sailboat, and maybe I can arrange something with them for you. I have some friends visiting from the mainland and we were thinking of going out scuba diving. Maybe we can all go out together."

That did sound like fun! Don and I looked at each other and winked. "Great idea!" he said. I chimed in and could hardly believe our luck.

Carl turned out to be the neighbor who was planning to lease this house. Linda and her partner had decided to go back to the mainland in a few months, and Carl had come over to check on a few things. What a meeting! A few days later everything was ready to go.

Meanwhile we met Carl's other friends: Suzanne, an amazing psychic, Damian, and Donna, the artist who had designed the cards that went along with wonderful book, *The Mayan Oracle* by Ariel Spilsbury & Michael Bryner.

After buying some food for our trip we arrived at the pier. Here we met a woman who had done a lot of dolphin research, and we were also introduced to the captain of the sailboat, Kathleen. Carl and Damian wanted to go scuba diving off the boat, and the rest of us were hoping for dolphins. Soon after we got onto the boat we began talking with the dolphin researcher—Roberta Quist-Goodman.

Wisdom of the Dolphins

This was too good to be true! She was helping Kathleen as a mate, hefting up the sails and getting us out of the harbor. As soon as we had some quiet time, I saw Don walk over to Roberta and start talking with her, and asking her questions. I could tell by the hand and body movements she made that she was describing experiences that had deeply moved her.

Gently, I nudged my way over to the two of them and started listening in. Here was Roberta Quist-Goodman, the woman I had read about in Lana Miller's book who had done the telepathic experiments with John Lilly's dolphins, Joe and Rosie. What coincidence! I was excited to hear more of her stories. Not too many researchers had the ability for telepathy, let alone considered telepathy a fact of life.

34

We were sitting on the bow of the sailboat and listening enraptured to Roberta's stories. "One night after I was getting ready to go home," she told us, still excited by the memory of her experience, "I felt like showing the dolphins some of our human world. If they could indeed understand what I mentally sent them from a distance, as had seemed to be the case with Joe and Rosie, maybe they would also be good at remote viewing. So that evening I sat by the pool and in my mind invited the dolphin Terry to mind-link with me.

"Suddenly I felt a shift in myself, as if someone went piggyback on my mind. When I got up to go home, everything I looked at had different meaning to me. As I met people I noticed how strangely we interacted. The distance we humans hold in our minds and bodies was noticeable. I had wanted to show the dolphins what our world looks like, and I felt like I was succeeding. Prior to this experience I had felt sad leaving the dolphins at the research pools but now I could take them home with me.

"They were so much a part of my life that I often felt closer to the dolphins than to humans. Every day they taught me something precious. I learned to trust, to rely on my feelings. Thinking back on the fact that a dolphin could ride piggyback on my mind, I am still awed. Consider what that potentially means for all of us. We can link across time and space, share insights from each other's worlds; maybe we can even space travel like this instead of using cumbersome spaceships."

As she talked, I thought of aliens, who could be regarded as inter-dimensional travelers that had learned to intersect with the physical world.

Roberta pulled me back into her story: "One time the dolphins took me swimming in circles in their pool. Joe took the lead and we went round and round. Then something strange and amazing happened. It was as if Joe had enveloped us in a glass bubble, and I felt like I was in a spaceship. We were traveling around the pool at high speed, but I felt absolutely no effort, and I could no longer feel the water touching me. Had we shifted into another frequency, which made it effortless to swim? Later I experienced the same effortlessness in the ocean." She paused.

I thought back to videotape footage on dolphin research I had seen some time ago. In it researchers studied the speed and endurance of dolphins. Regarding their energy capacity and output, there thus far seems to be no explanation for how they can perform as they do. Perhaps they tap the Chi energy, or maybe they utilize frequencies from other dimensions.

"That day they took me into a different dimension," Roberta added.

I loved it. Here was a person who had worked for years in close contact with dolphins under John Lilly's guidance, and she had managed to break through the intense barrier of communication via her inner senses.

"Dolphins love the frequency of ecstasy," Roberta continued. "If you want to call in the dolphins you have the best chance by heightening your own frequency. Go as high as you can; love as much as you can; send out joy and appreciation, and then let go. See the results you want in front of you; be in the experience as if it is already happening, that will generate the best results."

Ecstasy is indeed a carrot in front of our human noses. I thought of how wonderful I feel when people look at my inner self with its glory and beauty. How we blossom when we see the deepest truth of each other! At the core, if we just know how to look, we always find the soul's beauty. But to say kind things with a real sense of heart requires that we open ourselves, which makes us feel vulnerable. The rewards, however, the feelings of joy and the potential of ecstasy, are beyond words.

"There are so many dolphin stories to tell you," she started again, this time with a noted shift in her voice. "I'd love to tell you about instances of telepathy, otherworldly moments, intimacy, lessons in trust, and hard-hitting confusion and frustration because I could not use words with the dolphins. I would love to pass on to you the joy of holding a totally relaxed dolphin in my arms, of kissing, stroking, and hugging him or her. I remember the trust as a dolphin grasped my arm in her very sharp teeth and pretended to lunge, yet did not, testing my willingness to trust and let go. I also remember lying on the bottom of the pool and watching a dolphin jump into the air and dive down straight for my forehead, veering off just before impact. I remember the unique magical games that were never repeated.

"The precision and grace of their movements touched my soul forever. I remember being in a dolphin-created whirlpool, like a tornado, but yet they never touched me, missing me with precision. I was awed by them winking at me just before losing eye contact while swimming by me eleven times in a row—maybe to let me know they had caught onto the game I had come up with. It meant to me they were saying 'I love you,' and they responded to my telepathic request for a game with an exactness that left me startled.

"They were able to untrain years of responses in a single lesson. They gave me gifts of silence, tears of recognition, laughter at novel behavior. Through the years, I spent hours and hours wondering about them, trying, and hoping to communicate, to understand, to know. I remember a dolphin going limp in my arms as I breathed the last breath with her, her body in total surrender.

"I rejoice at the memory of a dolphin sucking my face with her blowhole, giving me dolphin kisses; at a dolphin stroking my legs with feather light touches. Once I visualized an object several inches in front of Terry and she began sonaring it.

"As my heart is touched by dolphins, I see grace becoming art, beauty becoming joy, as we are intertwining as one. Love fills my heart after years of dormancy. Hope pervades my mind after years of pessimism.

"Life opens to us in layers. I only wanted to swim with dolphins, take them to the open sea, have them take me to their pods. Instead they took my life for a ride I could not have imagined. I realize we have been communicating all along; I just need to expand my definition of language. Words are not the only way.

"I found a key to deeper levels of communication, which I learned from my interaction with dolphins. It comes through the elements of friendship, trust, and desire. Within the context of friendship, we can open up to new and expanded levels of communication. It happened naturally with dolphins; I loved each one I met. With humans it has come only with difficulty. I am just beginning to learn to apply what I know. How can I find the same quality of joy, trust, excitement, love, and desire with humans that I experienced with dolphins? Trust is difficult. The desire's not there. I wish I could feel with humans what I have felt with dolphins.

"My relationship with my daughter, though, has surpassed that with dolphins. With her I used the imagery I had learned from the dolphins and refined it. My "significant other" has also taken me places dolphins have not. As a community, can humans approach the closeness of dolphins? Through dolphins I came to believe in Heaven and it is through humans that we will bring Heaven to Earth."

We were moved and tears filled our eyes. She had seen worlds that are possible, and I wondered when humans would evolve enough to have the kind of Heaven that dolphins seemed to have already manifested. Some days it felt like we were only a shift of attention away from Heaven; other days it felt like it was eons away.

35

As Roberta shared her feelings and stories, the rest of our group formed a circle around her. Before we started our sailing journey, Kathleen intended for us to become akin, in mind, to a dolphin pod. Now we were starting to gather together, interwoven by invisible rays of light.

I sat in silence as the waves of Oneness came washing over us. The Mayan Oracle became our fulcrum, and we each drew cards for insight into our next steps in life. The cards brought our attention closer to the deeper energies in our lives and to moving in harmony with energies working through us. My card was about entering a new level of initiation, and I wondered what that would bring.

We spent the day closely sharing moments of truth with each other. We enjoyed deeply felt "flow" and ease, dances in the water and in spirit, snorkeling, and scuba diving, but on this day there were no dolphins. Only dolphin people and a spirit of Oneness blessed our day.

That night we all celebrated Damian's birthday at a Thai restaurant. As we gathered in a big circle around the dinner table I noticed how we were starting to slip into our "normal" social behavior of chitchatting. During the day we had been out of our ordinary context of "how to do things," but here, back on land, we reverted to our normal behavior.

Carl and Roberta were sitting across from me, and Don sat next to me. I remembered my encounter with Carl the first morning after my meditation. "Why not have our entire group see each other's beauty and brilliance?" I wondered and made the suggestion to the group. Everyone liked the idea, and I explained the rules.

"Let's start by telling each person one thing we appreciate about them. One person will be "it," and everyone else will go around in a circle and share his or her appreciation." We would do this three times for each person.

I looked at Roberta and appreciated her for opening her heart and telling us of her world, her triumphs, and her tribulations. I could hardly see Carl for all the Go Pal Das energy surrounding him, and in my sharing I really spoke both to him and Go Pal Das.

I felt a deep appreciation for his relentless spirit of bridging the inner light to the outer world, for his being so luminous, and for opening his spirit so easily to anyone who was willing to look high enough. His eyes shone in a turquoise blue and were brimming with tears. In a transfixed moment he spiraled up again with me and bowed in his spirit, we twined into One and I saw the picture Roberta had drawn with her words earlier that day of intertwining with a dolphin.

Here in this context of openness, appreciation, and the ability to see the deeper truth of each soul, I understood what Roberta meant when she said she learned from dolphins how a deeper level of communication can be reached when we are in a space of openness and trust. Carl's soul and mine hung suspended in another world, which allowed for the boundaries to evaporate for a brief moment in time.

Next was Don. As I looked at his luminous eyes, which had equally filled with tears as he watched the beauty of my sharing with Carl, I was speechless. Our spirits soared instantaneously on the wings of Soul into worlds of Light. God's presence in All-that-Is became profoundly palpable.

It was as if we journeyed into a hyper-dimension where our souls became One to such a degree that we burst out on the other side of creation in a fountain of light. Maybe this fountain of light was a white hole on the other side of a black hole.

By joining this way, we continually affirmed our willingness to surrender, opening ourselves to the highest frequency of union, harmony, and creation. Wasn't this what people hoped to experience by joining in lovemaking, a union of two into one? Wasn't this the way we "created" babies? Perhaps the universe carries a hidden key within its own matrix, that of unifying after it has individuated and creating from this unification new worlds of joy and learning.

Aligning with the center of creation is the key to aligning ourselves with our higher innate energies, with our purpose. As I had come to find out through the "Living From Vision" course, it is this alignment in oneness with the center of creation that makes creation of any kind possible.

As I looked into Don's eyes, our inner vision attuned to the subtle breezes of our journeying spirits, and we were filled with love.

The evening became magical and turned from a normal dinner to an ecstatic dance of seeing into the higher fields of creation. This was a way of bringing Heaven to Earth, simply by shifting our attention.

That night we went into a deep, satisfying sleep. The next day we were to go on a Zodiac ride to see if we could find dolphins.

36

The early morning doves cooed their songs as we rose from our sleep. After breakfast Don went to help Carl and our bed-and-breakfast host Dan fix the hole in the Zodiac while I sat down for my morning meditation. Contacting the dolphins inwardly before trying to meet them in physical form seemed beneficial, so I centered myself in my breathing and tuned my antennas to the dolphins.

In my mind I slowly rose above the coast line off Kihei where we would be taking the Zodiac. As I sent my rays of light to commune with the dolphins, letting them know that we were coming, I suddenly sensed that they were receiving my thought signals. It was as though I were sending out a line of light that was received and then sent back as a satisfying reflection.

The feeling was one of completion, similar to looking into your lover's eyes and sensing the subtle shift when they look back at you. A gentle smile runs across his or her face, lighting up their eyes. I knew and felt that the dolphins and I had made contact. Again I sent greetings to the "head" energy of the pod that I was hoping to see on our Zodiac ride.

Next I sent the thought image of us wanting to connect with the pod, possibly close to shore. At this point the dolphin mind sent me a jolting response. "No way are we going to swim over your way! Between our pod and you is a huge shark." No, they did not want to cross that dangerous line.

So much for my attempt at inviting the dolphins to see us. But then again, it was probably all in my head, and what does imaginary communication really prove anyhow?

With these thoughts in mind I rose from my meditation and we got ready to launch our Zodiac, which meanwhile had been fixed. Carl, Dan, Don, and I left in great anticipation of finally seeing dolphins in their element. The ride along the coast line was bumpy with our speedy little boat bouncing off the waves. The sun was rising high in the sky, and we skipped along the surface of the water like a walnut shell.

Carl stood at the back of the Zodiac manning the helm like a true captain. The sun shone from behind him and illuminated his windblown blond hair like a crown of light. Go Pal Das came to my mind again, and I started raising my vibration. I sensed my own field of light becoming brighter and helped the process by pretending to see filaments of light all around me, permeating each one of us at all times.

As I raised my eyes to meet Carl's, I saw into his soul. Billions of little rays of light were exchanging back and forth from his Source to mine, and a bridge of light arched from our eyes to the inner realms. The sun at the top of his head only added to the surrealistic perception that "we are made up of ecstatic rays of light," and suddenly the energy form the top of my head started connecting with his. A fountain of light engulfed us, and the fountain on top of my head started exploding. It was ecstatic! The closest way of describing this feeling is likening it to an orgasm from the top of my head. We both stood utterly still in our minds, beholding the wonder two humans can experience.

Do the dimensions of ecstasy open to us when we're willing to allow oneness into our heart? If so, we can choose to experience these states whenever we want. The biggest hurdle to maintaining this experience for long periods of time is the requirement that we keep our emotional "house" clean.

Here was Carl, a man who had done me no wrong, with whom I had no previous experience of pain, disappointment, or built-up anger. If there had been any of the latter, I would have had to clean my wounds and create a healing with him; otherwise I probably would not have been as willing to open my energy field to experience this ecstasy.

This type of cleaning requires a lot of commitment, commitment to staying in relationship through times of trouble, to extending feelings of understanding, and not just making peace in order to avoid conflict. Unless we really understand and feel understood, the sand kernels of misunderstanding turn into brick walls instead of being what they are meant to be; kernels to be turned into pearls of wisdom.

Don and I have spent countless hours over the years cleaning our emotional "house." We battled wills until we came to the point that we knew we had the other's best interest in mind, even if it meant admitting to one another that we were at fault. By being willing to be honest with ourselves and each other we increased our capacity to love, to honor, and to care for one another. But here on the boat I had experienced the luxury of an innocent beginning. No painful memories were in the way of opening my field up so intensely.

I tried to keep in mind the warning that Go Pal Das had given me. I was not to get attached to this particular person, even if he said exactly the same words that Go Pal Das would say to me. Carl was here to bridge the inner and outer world so that Go Pal Das and I could meet. It was an honor.

While I was still in my inner reverie, Dan noticed that water was entering our rubber boat from the bottom. We needed to stop and bail the water out and check to see if the hole in the boat's bottom was serious or not. Immediately I pulled my attention back into the three-dimensional world, and we quickly got to the task. While bailing the water out of the boat, I suddenly heard a big splash and turned to see what it was.

"A dolphin!" I thought. "Oh no, this one is huge! It doesn't make the exhalation sound so typical of dolphins. It has a straight, triangular dorsal fin, not curved like dolphins' and this one was . . . alone!"

Dolphins normally travel in groups, or at the very least with one or two others. "This one is a huge shark!" I suddenly realized.

I remembered my morning meditation. Had I indeed heard the right communication? That was almost too hard to believe. Was I really beginning to hear dolphins correctly? At least in some instances my telepathic communications seemed to verify themselves.

How, other than through experience, could I confirm, at least to myself, that telepathy with dolphins was possible and not solely the result of my happy and active imagination? Maybe this experience was yet another stone in the bridge over the gap of silence between humans and dolphins. If I could do it, so could many others. If telepathy worked with dolphins, it surely must work with all other beings as well.

I noticed how my own intuition had dramatically increased since I had been doing the imagery work. Others also told me of the increase in their own intuition as a result of imaging.

By listening to the language of images we can enter into a new world, one in which the walls of logic give way to a fluid reality, one in which we create and learn first on the inside and then manifest our thoughts and visions in the outside world, one in which we can experience the utmost joy, love, and Oneness, the true nourishment of our souls.

Somehow, in a roundabout way, this day had been a great dolphin day. I felt the presence of the dolphins' mind, heard the message and found confirmation. I felt that I was getting closer to the heart of communion with dolphins.

37

The following morning at daybreak we got up and readied ourselves for an adventure. It appeared that it was going to be hot, and I welcomed the cool breeze of the early morning caressing my skin. Roberta had told us about a bay on the island of Lanai where the dolphins visit regularly. Today we were going to take a boat ride over to the island, and with a bit of luck the dolphins would be there as well.

At the dock where the ferry left, we joined two other women we had met days earlier. Sensitive and adventuresome, both were beaming at us when we arrived. Quickly a giddy teenage mood came over the four of us, and we were ready for anything.

Once on the boat, we settled down and shared stories of how life had led each one of us to desire swimming with dolphins in the wild. Granted, the trials and tribulations had been many. It would have been much easier to go to a pool with captive dolphins and be entertained by the performance, but something in each one of us shook at the thought of it.

As a human, I certainly would not want to be caged in a cell too small for my needs, have to hold still while aliens touched my skin, or let myself be petted by them. Nor did I want to put any other being on this planet through this experience. Instead, each of us in our group preferred to undergo the trials of nature, learn about the natural rhythms of coincidence, and explore the hidden mysteries of natural attraction and communion.

Halfway to the island, Don and I felt drawn to meditate and let the dolphins know that we were coming. In the silent world of my images I had learned that what I saw within was often synchronistically happening in the outer world. I discovered that I pre-created my outer circumstances by the focus I held. We seem to tune in to specific frequency bands, much like we pick a radio station, and it felt like I could choose to enter Heaven on Earth as one of the many options. Heaven on Earth and the dolphins were synonymous to me.

Suddenly I felt the response from the dolphin pod. It was as if my Morse code had been answered, and I saw the dolphin's presence enter my inner field of vision. How did I know that this was a real connection and not just a fantasy? Certainly by trial and error I had learned to notice the difference.

Largely the "Living From Vision" course had taught me to utilize imagery in my daily life, and I got a clearer sense about when I was making things up and when things were "real." Don had helped me immensely. He was willing to be absolutely honest with me and let me know if my hunches had been accurate or not.

It had taken some time to come to the level of trust where he and I dared to admit to each other our innermost fantasies and little inconsistencies, admitting to mistakes we might have made. But in the long run our trust and honesty were a yardstick by which we could gauge whether we were making things up or if they were real perceptions.

Telepathy happens all the time between people, but it takes courage to let another person know the truth. Often we don't want to be rejected and therefore choose to fit in by not saying something or by pretending that what we feel is not really happening, since it might be socially incorrect or too frightening.

Don and I had worked many years at allowing our inner truth to be heard, even if it meant that one or the other didn't like it. After much learning, we came to see that we can find sympathy and understanding for almost everything. It did require that we ourselves were honest with our own natural feelings. As long as our highest aspiration is located in God and we have each other's best interest in mind, honesty is the best medicine for intimacy and vicariously also for telepathy.

As soon as I felt the dolphins strongly in my meditation, Don started nudging my hand. "Look, they came to greet the boat!" he whispered. We got up and looked over the railing. I couldn't help but feel waves of joy rushing over me. It was as if a higher energy field had entered my world, as if a rush of angel wings was touching my heart. Here we were, awed at the impeccable timing, moved to tears by the presence of these beings who spoke the inner language of telepathy and seemed to be able to penetrate the worlds of dreams.

As soon as the boat docked, the four of us quickly walked the short distance to the beach to see if more dolphins were in the bay. I could hardly believe our luck when indeed a whole pod of dolphins was visible from the shore. We saw wave upon wave of dorsal fins coming out of the water.

As quickly as we could, we put all our gear on and ran into the water. The waves were quiet and swimming felt easy. With dolphins in sight my fear of water disappeared, and all I could think about was being near these majestic beings.

Roberta had told us that the best way to get a dolphin's attention was to enter into a state of ecstasy. That was easy to say. Here I was paddling as fast as I could to get to the dolphins, and in the midst of this frenzy I needed to feel ecstasy!

I took a moment to slow down by simply hanging in the water, bobbing in the waves. I breathed slower and imagined that I was entering the realms of Heaven. I became aware of beams of sunlight streaming into the water past my body, giving the underwater world a super-luminous and otherworldly look. I felt as if I were swimming in a sea of love, light, and ecstasy with no effort on my part other than holding my attention on the super-luminous space around and within me.

As if out of nowhere, dolphins passed underneath me. Gracefully and in total harmony they passed below me like a wave of silent dancers. It was as if a veil had been lifted and I finally saw the dolphins I had been waiting for.

A deep wave of joy flooded through me, and I felt like bowing to the dolphins. With great reverence I sent my greetings, much like I would to any master. To my surprise I got a greeting back with a message that sounded like, "We are all equals and we have mutual respect for you."

And then they were gone as quickly as they had appeared. Had I heard the message correctly? Imaginary communication seems to be the way to bridge the gap of silence between humans and dolphins. All the previous "coincidences" with the dolphins, the meditations and telepathic transmissions, that had proved true, had been part and parcel of learning to trust my inner ears.

I wanted to know so much more. Again I went into the space of inner joy and into a state of awe, reverence, fulfillment, and gratitude and imagined being in the midst of a pod of dolphins. As soon as I held the feeling/thought of being in the midst of the pod, a whole group swam around me again. This time they seemed to check me out a little closer and must have determined that I was okay because they circled to the side and didn't just take off.

I wanted to know if dolphins had a concept of God, and I summoned up my thinking process as best I could to send out a question that sounded like: "Hi, dearest ones, how do you connect with God; what is your way of understanding the life-giving energy?"

Instead of a description I got an answer that took me into the experience of being the answer from the inside out. It was as though the pod of dolphins and I were simultaneously in the ocean as well as in a field of God's presence. The space around us expanded into cosmic dimensions, and we were forms, bodies in the water, and at the same time Oneness with All-that-Is. I "saw" a heightened space extending way up into the cosmos as well as surrounding every particle of my essence. Humans, water, dolphins, God's creation—we all are One.

With this "living" answer came the request to show my human perception of being with God. As best I could, I sent an image/experience of how I connect with God. I sent the concept of being in alignment with the highest Source I could possibly imagine. I imagined a wide beam of light extending from this Source to me and through me. Then I became this light source, losing my sense of self-identity, letting All-that-Is wash through me and become me, finally pulling the presence of the Source back through my physical world into the ocean and all I felt within it.

As I passed this image/answer to the dolphins I noticed a very strange effect. In my ecstasy imagery, I noticed that the dolphins had almost stood still beneath me. Dolphins never stand still, since they always swim, keeping constantly in motion.

I stretched out my arms as if to pass all the information through my whole body, letting the inner light flow out my arms as if in prayer to the sky, but now facing into the ocean, blessing the dolphins and sending feelings of gratitude for being in their presence.

When I let go of my intense focus, the dolphins kicked strongly with their tail flukes and off they went. Had they stood still as we held divine communion? Did they hear me and leave perfectly in time with the end of our communion? This was blissful beyond my wildest imagination; only my dreams were this good.

Approximately seventy spinner dolphins were swimming around us in the bay. The other two women and Don had spread out to have their own experience. Without dolphins in the water I would have stayed close to Don, hanging on for dear life, but with the dolphins around me I felt the same familiar feeling of love, safety, and at-home-ness that

I had felt at the secret beach on Kauai. The dolphins had been chirping and sonaring us as they came near, and at times I could hear them before I could see them, especially when they came from behind. I felt safe, but couldn't explain how their presence gave me such a strong feeling of trust and safety.

The more often they came around us, the more they dared to swim near us. Not only were they developing trust, but so were we. After all, they were the biggest swimming beings in the water I had ever experienced other than humans, and they were definitely more powerful than I was.

We were trying to get to know each other, and I had a strong sense of respect for the dolphins. Luckily no one in our group had the "see and dash" attitude that I had noticed at the secret beach on Kauai. Instead, all of us worked via the inner dimensions of atunement, through the use of imagination.

At this point I noticed how the dolphins came my way, and I turned until I was going in the same direction they were. I angled toward them, gently easing my swimming pattern to fit theirs. They seemed to like this way of easing into their swimming pattern better than other approaches.

The next time they swam by me I tried to swim quickly, keeping my fins as silent as I could, since they seemed to be speedier than before. Then the most curious thing happened. They swam beneath me, and this time I tried to keep up with them, kicking hard. Suddenly I felt like I was flying with them. I was swimming slightly above them near the surface, as five of them swam below, and somehow I felt like I didn't need to exert *any* energy anymore. An invisible envelope of silent, speedy gliding held me in rapture.

We swam as One! No effort was needed on my part. I simply felt like I was gliding at high speed, outside of time and space, in the same envelope of energy with the pod of dolphins. This long moment of being one pod together was absolutely magnificent, a gift from the dolphins. This was Heaven!

38

As none of our group made any attempt to go back to shore I kept on swimming. I wanted to see if I could send a message to which the dolphins would respond. From the depth of my heart I wanted to know more about the dolphin mothers and their babies.

Roberta had told us that the young dolphins swim at their mother's side for several years, staying especially close in the first year, nursing much like humans would. The little ones learn how to hold their breath as the dolphin mothers hold them underwater for longer and longer periods before allowing them to breathe.

Because of their sonar and apparent telepathic ability, the dolphins can see the internal bodily conditions of other beings. This helps the dolphins to know when their young ones need to breathe, as well as how others around them feel.

As soon as I held the image of dolphin moms and babies in my mind, a whole group came around with their babies. Maybe they had not swum around me earlier to make sure that the babies were safe, but now they were right in front of me. I was moved beyond words. Here in absolute synchronistic timing with my inner images I was led into the midst of the dolphin nursery. The little dolphins behaved much like human babies would. Curious, they swam a little closer to see me, sometimes a bit lopsidedly, "waddling" around like toddlers, not yet having total body control and not yet having learned all the social protocols.

When a little one was behaving too riskily, he or she was called to order by his or her mother, and I had to laugh underwater. Watching the dolphins reminded me of the way humans raise children. Humans correct children's behavior when they talk to a stranger with a little too much curiosity. I sent love to the moms and tried to send images of humans with children.

I don't know how long I had been swimming back and forth with the dolphins, but suddenly I heard loud and clear a message in my head. "Get out of the water; swim back to the shore, now! You only have a certain amount of strength to get back, and you cannot afford to keep swimming with us any longer."

Wow, what a message! It had only taken a split second to hear all this, and yet it was a lot of information.

I stuck my head out of the water to see if anyone else was ready to go back, when to my surprise Don and one of the women who had swum near us stuck their heads out at the same time. "Did you hear what I heard?" I asked.

"That we are to swim back?" the other woman said.

"Yes, I heard the same thing!" Don added in awe.

"Well guys, I think we better listen," I said. "Let's head back." The dolphins seemed to have turned away from us and were swimming seaward, which made it easier for us to let go of them.

Slowly and steadily we swam back, breathing rhythmically and deeply. I watched the small beach grow in size ever so slowly and became aware that my left ankle was getting painfully sore. No kidding, the dolphins must have known more about me than I did. Now that I was more aware of myself and my body, I noticed how exhausted I felt. A surge of panic came over me, and I worried about making it back to the beach. "What if I can't make it? What if my legs cramp?" I really felt exhausted and weak.

"Don't let your mind run astray right now," I told myself. "Keep focusing; you can do it." Steadily I paddled my legs and made some headway. The sand came into view beneath me, and I started anchoring my sight on the ripples in the sand, inching myself forward. Then I heard the dolphins' sonar from behind me. "Those tricksters," I thought. "They knew that we might not have gone back to the beach if they had stayed right around us."

Rather, the dolphins had turned as if to go out to sea and only returned when they were certain that we were heading back to the beach.

Finally I made it close to shore, took off my fins, and got ready to get out of the water. The waves were very small, and I was sure I would make it to the beach without a problem. How I had misjudged my energy! As I tried to step out of the water, my legs simply collapsed. Gravity was more than I could handle at the moment. I caught myself and crawled slowly to the safety of the sand, fully collapsing under the shade of a palm tree.

The dolphins must have known with absolute precision the level of my available energy and the amount of strength it would take to get back. Don and the other woman reached the beach at the same time, and we marveled at the exact sameness of the message all three of us had heard.

Had the dolphins not only assessed our energy correctly

but also communicated with us intentionally? If so, we needed to overhaul our understanding of communication and include levels that we as humans had previously considered "not possible" or even "unscientific." How had I been able to hear the dolphins? What had we each done to be able to do so? What could we as humans do to learn the art of telepathy?

As we lay under the tree the fourth woman came to shore. She had been swimming a bit further away from us and had suddenly gotten the feeling that it was time to go back to the beach. Obviously not everyone heard "messages." To some people the messages came in the disguise of "having a feeling," or simply being moved to do something.

I noticed an increase in my telepathy and intuition with the increase in my imagery work. Seminar participants who practiced transforming old images into new ones, made the same observation. Their intuition, telepathy, and precognition seemed to increase and they saw the bending of time and space give rise to anomalies in the fabric of creation. Imagination seemed to be the key, as well as learning to take the images seriously and learning to distinguish between fantasy and "real" imagination. Once we entered the domain of communicating with the inner realms via our imagination, we were on the way to discovering the central path to the fountain of creation.

As we lay under the palms resting contentedly, I noticed how happy I felt. The pattern of light shining through the leaves swaying in the wind created a surreal feeling of Heaven. There was meaning even in the breeze, purpose in just being here. A brighter light was now shining through the palms than before, a light that answered my deepest longing for meaning. I relaxed deeply in the beauty that seemed to pour out of every fiber of everything I looked at. I saw the beauty, and the beauty saw me, and that was meaningful enough in and of itself. Were we conscious beings within creation, in order to awe and marvel at creation? I was certainly filled to the brim with gratitude and bliss.

After our rest we slowly started sharing one word here and one sentence there about our experience, our feelings about life, and some simply giddy things. We were open to one another, people who had been strangers until not long ago. I felt as if we constituted a group-mind, being bonded almost in a cellular way. My inner walls of protection were down; my appreciation of each of us as valuable beings had increased, and all we had done was jump into the water and swim with dolphins.

Suddenly, as if we all had the same thought, we decided to get up and explore the nearby hotel. In a seaside tea room there was supposed to be free afternoon cookies and tea, and besides we could take a dip in the beautiful outdoor pool.

The path up to the hotel overlooked the bay, and the ocean sparkled like a jewel. We passed by the pool, promising ourselves a sunset swim later, and made our way to the restaurant. Just coming for free cookies when we weren't even staying at the hotel didn't seem fair, so we decided to check out the menu. As good as our intentions were, not much on the menu was anywhere near our price range. Finally we decided on some wild mushroom soup with bread and salad. The linens, the crystal glasses, the silverware, the waiters who were accustomed to serving in a gracious style, the view into the tropical garden—all felt like a gift from Heaven.

Sitting in a most unusual setting, we all felt absolutely grateful. The wild mushroom soup was beyond words. The cookies and tea, now justly deserved, made for a delicious dessert.

The sun started setting and its still warm rays beckoned us to dip into the pool. As I stepped into the turquoise water the last rays of the sun sent golden sparkles over my face. I was in bliss. Ecstasy came over me in a rush, cascading from a fountain within me. A simple shift in my way of seeing and I was in Heaven. God, Oneness, and Love all filled my heart, and I glanced over at Don who had followed me into the pool.

The world almost stood still. Although the surroundings looked the same, one might have called this world we were experiencing by a different name. We simply looked at everything as if it were Heaven, as if everything were made of gold. As I looked around I could see that everything was surrounded by many levels of light. My gaze penetrated a particularly beautiful light, and I felt my heart sing the same beautiful melody of light. "Who else was seeing beauty in their world?" I wondered.

Dolphins have a knack for inducing this state of being, and that was perhaps the reason we could call them by entering into a state of quiet ecstasy, like Roberta had told us. Like attracts like. And maybe we lift veils from hidden treasures by shifting into subtler dimensions, opening the doors to Oneness, love, and miracles.

With each image transformation I did, I had to enter into the center of creation, a central space in my mind that was the gateway to the zone of time- and space-shifting.

39

After dinner, we meandered back to our camping spot by the beach and nestled into our tents, under our covers. So far, this had been the best dolphin experience we'd had, and we slept deeply and very contentedly.

Soon the time came to leave Maui and return to our world on the mainland. During our last few days on Maui, Carl showed our little group some beautiful hidden places on the island. Glistening waterfalls cascading into deep green pools gave us the supreme feeling of being in paradise. We sat naked in the hot sun high up on the cliffs before jumping into the depths of the cool water below. I tried hard to remember that Carl was not necessarily only Carl for me. Go Pal Das continued speaking to me through him, and I was spellbound when I heard Carl saying things word for word that Go Pal Das had told me inwardly, in my mind.

After our return home, I noticed a definite change in the way Carl spoke and communicated with me on the telephone. He was himself again. Gone was any similarity to Go Pal Das, and in one way I was glad.

Don and I were returning to our business, writing and recording guided-imagery tapes, working on books, recording music, and running our mail-order business for innovative healing tools. We export some of our equipment, and we've been happy to see that at least in some countries the truth can be said about the effects these tools have. One instrument has helped people eliminate depression and addictions. Years ago I went through an intense period of stress followed by a year-long depression and only came out of it through the use of one of these instruments. What a blessing it had been! We have received letters from many people, thanking us for these tools, telling us how the tools had saved their lives and their hopes, and thus we feel like our work has made a difference in the world.

The world of the dolphins made its way into our daily thinking and nightly dreaming. One night shortly after our return from Maui I had a peculiar dream that reminded me of the one with the whales.

Don, Roberta, and I were walking on a sidewalk, and three dolphins came racing out of the ocean, flopping themselves right onto the pavement in front of us. We were horrified, quickly grabbed the dolphins, and threw them back into the water!

A few days later the oddest thing happened . . . again. I read the headlines of one of the newspapers as I walked past the store on my daily trip to the post office. Could I believe my eyes? Here was a story on dolphins who had beached themselves the previous day *and* who had been *successfully* returned to the water!

How much are our dreams tied into our daily living? Either I receive telepathic newspaper messages in my dreams, or we happen to act in other dimensions that have an effect on the physical world. I was beginning to believe in the possibility of the second idea. Maybe it was part and parcel of the "Dream Dolphin Training" I was receiving, gaining understanding of the deeper layers of truth about reality.

A couple of days later, Roberta called and I told her the story. She was puzzled. She wondered if I had picked up any other "daily news" in my dreams, but I hadn't. Not picking up other news in my dreams could be an indication of multidimensional work, unbeknownst to my conscious mind.

Roberta enjoyed hearing of our nightly work together but had called for a different reason. She wanted to tell us that one of the easiest places to swim with dolphins was off the island of Key West in Florida. A friend of hers had a boat and took people out into the open waters where a friendly pod of dolphins had been coming to meet him day after day, year after year. Roberta was due to be in Key West in a few months, and she wondered if we could visit with her. Since we had been given coupons by United Airlines for volunteering to be bumped off our previous Maui flight, the tickets to Key West were almost covered! What an invitation! Of course we would come!

We timed our trip to coincide with Roberta's arrival and soon were booked on as many trips on her friend's boat as possible.

Key West was hot and humid and had a distinctly Caribbean flair. We stayed at a very colorful bed-and-breakfast, which was surrounded by blooming tropical flowers, and had bright yellow book shelves and multicolored yarns on a weaving loom. Breakfast was a feast for the eyes and a delight for our taste buds, with many ripe tropical fruits, delicious homemade cakes and bagels, and freshly squeezed juices.

The first boat trip left at ten in the morning, we could

hardly wait for our departure. We reminisced with Roberta about the time we sailed from Maui trying to find dolphins and I got so seasick that I had sworn off any further boat rides. But this boat was different. Ron, the captain, had a catamaran, which held its balance much better.

We were six people plus Ron the captain. There was a mother and a father with their teenage daughter and the three of us. As we left the dock, I started deep alternate-nostril breathing. It is my way of creating a physical foundation for experiencing and holding a state of ecstasy in my body.

First I inhaled through my right nostril, holding the left nostril closed. As I did this, I visualized super-luminous light pouring into the top of my head; then I let my breath out through my left nostril, all the while flooding my whole body with light. As I continued alternate-nostril breathing, I felt more and more luminous. Slowly I started sensing the world of dolphins approaching.

Ilona Selke

40

As we drifted with our catamaran over the turquoise waters, our eyes scanned the horizon for signs of dolphin activity. The water was calm and the wind smelled salty. Although I had the feeling that dolphins were near I did not see any. I thought maybe the dolphins wouldn't show up for me this time; maybe they would show up for someone else today. To think like that made me feel a little sad.

"Quiet, Ilona", I told myself. "Remember to focus your energy on the result this feeling really wants." Quickly I identified the feeling of anxiety as butterflies in my stomach. I took the image-feeling "outside" myself and asked it what it really wanted. Instantly I perceived the image of unifying with the dolphins as the true underlying desire and before my inner eye I saw a brilliant light embracing the dolphin and me in communion. I thanked the butterfly image and let it become the image of what it really had wanted, *union with the dolphins*. I brought this new image to a common meeting place in my mind and let it go to work on my "outer" reality.

Suddenly I felt like I was being seen by a dolphin, yet I couldn't see any. A wave of joy rushed through me. Within a short time someone shouted from the front of the boat, "There they are!" as everybody became joyfully alert. The dolphins love to swim in the bow waves of the boat, and we got our first glance of the dolphin family.

"Hi Nick, hi Grandy!" the captain shouted into the water. He definitely tried to be loud enough so the dolphins could hear him. What excitement! Ron identified the dolphins to us by the marks they had on their dorsal fins or tail flukes. The "teenagers" were easy to tell apart. Sweetheart and Nick were at that time about seven and nine years old, the youngest of the pod.

There was Long-Tall, Hatchet, and Spur, very large male dolphins, and Grandy, the mother of Sweetheart and Nick. I was thrilled just to hang my head over the low railing and watch them turn slightly onto their sides to make eye contact with us. The feeling of being so close to the dolphins brought tears to my eyes. I felt an overwhelming joy at seeing them and could not help but feel blessed.

Soon we stopped the boat, put on snorkel gear and flippers, and jumped into the water. If the dolphins chose to be with us, they would come around us. If not, we wouldn't chase after them, as we wanted to honor the trust that Ron had built with the dolphins over time.

Still, I could hardly wait for my turn. Ron had his own wisdom about whom he wanted to go first, and we all surrendered to his plan. Roberta, Don, and I were to go into the water together. As we were getting ready we talked about being a pod and how dolphins were in constant contact with each other, always being part of a group.

Gently we lowered ourselves into the water, feeling the warmth touch our skin. This was pleasant. I like warm water! It wasn't deep, not more than twelve feet, and the sunlight lit the white sand underneath us.

Within moments several dolphins passed beneath us. "I

am home; these are my friends," I thought as my heart reached out to them. Tears filled my eyes inside my mask, and an intense emotion flooded through me. Even when I could not see any dolphins, I could still hear their echolocation and I felt their sonar touch my body. It was strange to "feel" sound touch my body. I felt *seen* in my emotions as well as in my form. Then the dolphins slid away as fast as they had come.

I remembered the dictum "Image the results you want," and in my mind I sent love to Sweetheart. Somehow my heart had caught onto him as I watched him from the railing. Now I sent the image of complete love to him, conveying a sense of total surrender, like a lover would.

Suddenly a dolphin dashed toward me and passed underneath me just to jump out of the water and arch into the air. Stunned, I stuck my head out of the water to see if the others on the boat had been able to see him jump, too.

"You must have said something amazing to him," captain Ron shouted. I blushed but luckily no one could tell, as I was hidden behind my pink mask.

As if Roberta, Don, and I had a telepathic link, the three of us simultaneously moved into an underwater ballet together, diving down and swirling about each other. For moments I lost all awareness of trying to be with the dolphins and simply enjoyed the three of us dancing together. That very moment several dolphins joined us in our union and gracefully wrapped themselves around and beneath us. Fully absorbed in this experience we were a sea of waves interlacing, yet never touching, ever so close. Huge, glistening gray bodies interwove with the feeling in our hearts and interacted with us as one mind. For a few moments we formed a human-dolphin pod, solely moved by our intuition, graced by love for one another.

As I came up for air the thought flashed through my mind that the dolphins must know exactly how we were moving because they were so agile, so close, so graceful. Our union felt like a gift from Heaven, and we could not have coordinated it any better. Maybe our attention on being a pod before we went into the water had prepared us to let go of our individual minds and become a pod for a moment. As if to reinforce our behavior, this small group of dolphins came around us just at that instant and joined us. Here we were, humans and dolphins diving as one, each willing to interact with the other, receiving the gift of union that crossed the boundaries of the gulf between our species.

After we came back onto the deck we were in absolute ecstasy. We sat with the parents and their teenage daughter, and I noticed how we formed a circle, how warm we each felt toward one another, and how much respect I felt for everyone. Was this part of the dolphins' gift to us?

I've noticed many times how people drop their judgmental mind when they start using imagery. The nonjudgemental mind does not think in terms of differentiation. It is able to see the whole picture, to recognize the deeper underlying patterns. Especially when the mind is focused on life-affirming energy there seems to be more light in a person's heart, and he or she is more willing to see the same in another.

Rachel, the daughter, was sharing how she would bring back to her school the understanding she had gleaned from swimming with the dolphins. She felt that deep insights were stimulated by being around them. She was excited by all her new ideas and feelings, and I honored her ancient soul. How blessed she was that her parents had the wisdom to allow this experience into her life, and now many more people were going to benefit from it!

Time was coming to an end for this morning's ride, and we were heading home, waving good-bye to the dolphins. We had started making friends with this pod of dolphins, and tomorrow we would all be back, no doubt.

41

The next afternoon we went out on the boat again. It definitely had been a test of patience waiting until the afternoon, but our bodies appreciated the rest. The humidity and the newness of everything surrounding us took time to get used to. For lunch we bought veggie sandwiches from a waterfront health food store. We spent some time watching the ever-changing clouds in the deep blue sky.

The dolphins had been active in the morning, Ron told us as we entered the boat where we were joined by a few more new people. My internal critic was not absentminded and noted that one guy in particular was not up to "my" taste. "Oh well," I thought and busied myself with stowing our sandwiches in the fridge.

Soon we were off and puttering toward the playing field of the dolphins. Apparently the dolphins knew the sound of Ron's boat and came by when they felt in the mood for interaction. "Were they going to be in the mood this afternoon after such an active morning?" I wondered.

My thoughts were not unfounded and we spent considerable time just sitting in the waves, looking and hoping. Then we saw *one* dolphin. It was Sweetheart, and Ron recognized him right away. A single dolphin was not going to be the best match for a group of six dolphin-anxious people. "Was this afternoon's trip to be in vain?" I wondered. Then a brilliant idea came to me.

I attuned myself to Sweetheart and simply felt like we could talk. If I were to give words to what I sent to him in thoughts and feelings, it would have sounded something like, "Hi Sweetheart, I see that you are here to play, but we are six people, and it really would be a lot more fun if we could all get to swim with a few more dolphins. Would it be possible for you to go and get some of your friends and family?" I thought he got it because I received an answer.

"Sure, I'll see if I can rouse them up and bring them here; I'll be back in fifteen minutes," Sweetheart beamed back.

"Great!" I thought. "Just don't tell anyone else what I heard, especially the part about fifteen minutes; they might think I'm nuts." With a dash Sweetheart was off and everyone else except me was disappointed. "Maybe it was true what I heard," I mused.

Lo and behold, I could hardly believe my eyes. Fifteen minutes later the whole dolphin gang was there. There was pregnant Grandy, Nick, Sweetheart, Long-Tall, Hatchet, and a few others. "This is for real; dolphins really communicate telepathically and even know how to keep time," I grinned to myself.

Now we all were in a mood for celebration! It had really looked gloomy, and there was no way to know for sure whether the dolphins were in the mood to play. Today my little request must have coincided with their willingness, and I was overjoyed.

We did all get to swim with the dolphins, taking turns to make sure that not too many of us were in the water at the same time. I practiced holding my breath a little longer and as I swam like I imagined a dolphin would, a group of three dolphins came into view underneath me in one sudden, swift movement. Kicking with flippers was exhausting, and I easily ran out of air. As if the dolphins knew my plight, I suddenly felt like I was taken again into that silent envelope of Oneness. With these three beings beneath me, we started gliding through the water together with great ease.

Gone was the effort; gone was the gasping for air. For one long moment in time we were one mind, one envelope of energy, one field of force. Then I heard in my mind that it was time for me to breathe, and I quickly swooshed upward to the silvery surface of the ocean. "Did you see that?" I shouted to the boat.

"Yeah!" Ron called back. "You were really cruising fast!"

So it wasn't just my internal sense, but I actually did go faster. Amazing! Could the dolphins create a field of energy flux around them and envelop another being into their force field, thereby increasing each other's physical strength? This experience underwater felt as close to being in another dimension, while still operating fully in this physical world, as I could possibly imagine.

Then in my inner sense of gratitude I sent a question to the dolphins, "Is there anything I can do to help you in any way?"

In an instant I got the picture of a mushroom cloud of sand going up in the water. Was it an image of bombs going off underwater? Was that still being done? For some reason I didn't think that anyone was detonating nuclear bombs underwater anymore. I searched in my mind. Did the Cubans, not too far from here, drop bombs? What could this image mean? Actually it was loud and clear, but I just couldn't fit it into my current knowledge of what was going on. Nor did I know how I could help.

That was the end of our trip, and we returned to the shore. I noticed how even the "unlikable guy" seemed so much more amicable and how we felt like one giddy pod of humans.

The gifts today were many, and I moved much closer to experiencing a multidimensional way of being with dolphins.

42

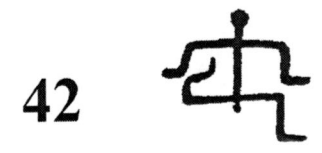

The next day we were inundated by a tropical storm and for hours were held captive by walls of rain. Needless to say, we did not go out on the ocean that day and anxiously wondered if the rain was ever going to stop. By late afternoon the dark thunderclouds disappeared and gave way to a glorious sunset. That evening we went to the famous boardwalk where Key West's creative artists display their talents. "Cooookies, really chocolate-loaded cooookies!" cooed a middle-aged lady from her bicycle storefront.

Mimes, men in chains, fire eaters, and craftspeople contributed to the entertainment! We enjoyed an African man the best. He sang beautiful heartfelt songs while playing his guitar. He was an older man, and his sweet voice filled the air. He sang with a maturity that only time and experience can bring.

The following morning Don and I were anxious to go out on the boat again. It was our last day. This time Roberta could not come with us. We were again a group of six people, and the sunny sky was promising. I did my breathing exercises again, as they really worked for me. I felt high like a kite simply from breathing slowly and with attention. Some time ago I met a man who was going to teach me a "very effective breathing technique, as taught by a lineage of Indian monks." I was so thrilled when I discovered that it was the same method Yogananda had taught and that it was also described by Itzak Bentov in his book *Stalking the Wild Pendulum*. This type of alternate-nostril breathing creates quite an altered state, especially when the breathing is combined with the image of absorbing luminous light.

As we came close to the place where our dolphin family usually played, I started thinking of our group on the boat as being one pod. "What would happen if I connected with all of us as One mind?" I wondered. I closed my eyes and expanded into the peace around me. In my mind's eye I rose up until I was floating above our boat.

Inwardly I reached a higher vantage point, and the kind of limits we know within physical confines dissolved. I was hovering in higher space and pretended in my mind that each of us on the boat could be seen as a shining star of light. I could sense the particular essence within each star. I felt great honor for each one, and as I did I imagined "us" in this space of inner union forming a circle, one that reached up into a star of Oneness.

"Oh my God," someone exclaimed, "look at that! There are almost fifteen dolphins here."

I opened my eyes. Unbelievable! The pod of dolphins had shown up out of nowhere, swimming in a perfect circle. Their noses and dorsal fins were floating visibly near the surface of the water, creating the image of a circle. As I broke my inner sense of concentration on our human one-pointed star, the dolphins disassembled out of their circle as well, floating around, some here, some there. I decided to see if envisioning the humans as a group-mind was in any way connected with this unusual swimming configuration of the dolphins.

I moved once again upward in my inner vision and attuned myself to the Oneness of our group. Again, I saw each of us represented by a star image and then felt all the stars unite into One. I quickly opened my eyes. Yes! Indeed! The dolphins had again formed a perfect circle to the right of our boat. Could this be real? They must be super, and I mean *super*, perceptive! I was awed.

The dolphins were swimming in a circle, making this circle visible to us by sticking a part of their body out of the water as they united into one floating ring. They could have been underwater as they usually are, in which case we would not have been able to see them. Was this a form of feedback for us, for me, so that I could understand the connection between the inner and the outer reality?

Next I thought of the ultimate experience! What would happen if I imagined the one-mind of the dolphins and the one-mind of the humans as overlapping, creating a giant one-mind of humans-dolphins? I felt a great amount of love for all of us here as I quietly sat down again.

The most amazing thing happened! In my mind I drifted up into the higher space and began to see the dolphins as a group of unified star beings at the same time as I saw the humans unify in a circle of stars. Then I pulled the images of the dolphins' star circle and the humans' star circle on top of each other, creating the sense of merging two circles.

As I did this I was enveloped by an intense feeling of ecstasy, unity, and love. Indescribably, I was lifted into a space of Oneness and the purest sense of intense Love and Life. It was sheer ecstasy, making me feel in perfect Oneness with God. Light pulsated through every cell and through all of us, now indistinguishable as One. I was in bliss.

To see if this new imagery had an effect on the dolphins' configuration, I sneaked a look at what had happened in the outside pod of physical dolphins. I was not anticipating what I saw.

Another pod of dolphins, about fifteen of them, and approximately thirty now all together, had suddenly appeared out of nowhere and formed a giant circle with the first pod. When I refocused my attention from the inner to the outer world, the dolphins split into two separate groups, floating strangely close to the surface, yet in two circular groups

Oh my, this was beyond belief! This was not a show, not a trick. The dolphins reflected to me the intense reality that our inner imagination is capable of co-creating. My imagination wasn't *just* in my own head; it clearly must have been felt by the dolphins as well, who were so gracious and fed the image back to us in the form of their symbolic swimming configuration.

Quickly I closed my eyes again. Was it just coincidence? I tried the same imagery again. Our uniting into One was again beyond words. It felt like the most earthshaking ecstasy possible, and I was being rewarded with the greatest amount of joy, bliss, and gratitude I could imagine, making me feel as close to enlightenment as I could fathom.

Curiosity got to me, and I opened my eyes. It had happened again! The two circles of dolphins had converged into one and started slowly breaking up after I let go of my focus. WE WERE ONE! Our imagination has effects that reach into the farthest crevices of our three-dimensional reality! Dolphins have a habit of showing up almost instantaneously in response to imagery, and the big group today showed up out of nowhere. Maybe the dolphins were teaching me, coaxing me into a certain imagery experience. But one thing was sure: *A greater reality was being accessed by humans and dolphins joining together.*

The circle of dolphins reminded me of the dream in which they encircled me and told me they were restructuring my energy system. Did the dolphins work as much in other dimensions as in the water? The dreams, telepathic communications, and now this "out-of-the-water" experience allowed me to enter into a new way of sharing with dolphins that reached beyond the confines of the physical world.

Slowly I felt guided into an understanding that would bridge the subjective and objective dimensions of life. Our imagination is truly so much more than just a function of cognition; it is a bridge into an "invisible" world. This is a world made of strands of Light, the web of life that is creating the very fabric of our solid-appearing world. Our imagination is interweaving within this fabric of Light, co-creating reality all the time. Where was I being led?

43

After this "high" in the inner dimensions I was glad to get into the pleasant waves of the water and swim with the dolphins. The physical energy output was a good balance to the internal intensity I had just experienced. With the warm sun reflecting on the water I welcomed the splashes of this liquid world.

As soon as Don, myself, and one other person slid into the water, the dolphins came right over to us, and we started our underwater ballet. Inches from my body the dolphins swam in a joyous frenzy. They had started becoming very lively and almost scared me by getting so close, but I relaxed and enjoyed their unusually close encounter with us.

A definite shift regarding how close the dolphins came to us had taken place. Had the dolphins checked us out the previous days? Each passing day they seemed to swim closer to us than the day before. Somehow that made sense. After all, that's how humans would approach a stranger, at first a little distant, then coming a bit closer each time. I also had the impression that the dolphins had sonared us from a distance, even while we were on the boat, checking us out.

After swimming for a while I noticed that Don had been gone for a considerable time now and looked around to find him. People on the boat helped me by pointing in his direction. Later he told me of the amazing time he spent with Grandy, the dolphin mom. She had taken a fancy to

Wisdom of the Dolphins

Don and singled him out, encouraging him to swim along with her, side by side, up and down, something even Ron found highly unusual. Don and Grandy swam together, communing and deepening their connection, sharing insights about the dolphin baby she was carrying within. After twenty minutes their sharing came to an end and Grandy gave a final big kick with her tail fluke before she dashed off. It was awesome for Don to be eye to eye with a dolphin as though they were friends.

The pregnant Grandy rubbed her heavy belly on the sand at times, often accompanied by two other dolphins. Later, when we were back on the boat, I felt moved to "bless" the new baby. I stood at the front of the boat where the low rail allowed me to see into the eyes of the dolphins swimming in the bow wave below us.

Mentally I let Grandy know that I was going to bless her and her baby with the highest state of awareness and energy I could generate and to my surprise she swam right over to where I was standing. With my hands outstretched and palms facing down, I focused on the highest beam of light I could imagine. As if I could see a beam reaching from the highest heaven, I imagined Grandy bathing in this stream of light. I held this intense focus for a couple of minutes and sensed that Grandy loved showering in the presence of this light. As soon as my attention broke and I let go of the imagery, she swam off. The feedback of her swimming away just as I let go of my imagery was invaluable. She had come over to me just as I started sharing the blessing with her and left the moment I stopped.

Dolphins seem to respond instantly to inner nudges,

something I think they tried to teach me in the next event that happened.

We were about ready to leave for the day. Ron was reeling in the ropes from the tow boards we had used earlier. Suddenly I felt a distinct *call* from a dolphin to jump into the water *now*, because one of them was on his way over to the boat. Ron had let some of our group jump into the water to get wet just before we were to leave. Since it had been up to Ron to decide who was to go into the water and who wasn't, I did what I was supposed to do: I asked him if it was okay for me to get into the water, too.

"No!" he said, while hinting at the fact that we were soon to leave anyway and that the dolphins were gone. At that moment, Spur, a big male dolphin came dashing out of the water, right near the back of the boat where I was sitting.

"Listen to your own authority; act more in alignment with the inner truths you know," came the message in my head.

I got this lesson clearly! There was nothing like a missed dolphin opportunity to act as a permanent memory marker. I became so aware of how we humans stifle our intuition. How many times had it been that I chose not to do something simply because it would not "fit in"?

Social rules, agreements, and ethics are good to have, as they allow us to live in a civilization where many different states of awareness and levels of ethics and accountability are present. We have at once a society where some people think nothing of stealing, while others feel the need to tell a sales clerk that he/she undercharged them.

At some point though, when one is willing to be

accountable, when one carries the ethics of life in one's heart, when one makes sure that one is working with the benefit of others in mind, when these standard laws of life have become internalized, then one starts being guided by yet a higher set of laws. These higher laws are equally real and have their own rhyme and reason. They take into account that one's sense of *self* and the laws of time and space have expanded. It is through our inner voice that we can hear these nudges.

Today with the dolphins around, I realized that I still needed to listen more to my inner voice.

Swimming with the dolphins so close today, with the circle of Oneness blessing my life and Don having had such an extraordinary experience with Grandy, I felt like I was in absolute paradise! The world was shifting, and I saw the imagery of the subjective world and the solid-appearing, objective outer world converging. If I could just figure out the meaning of the message the dolphins had sent me about the underwater bomb! It just didn't make any sense to me; not yet.

44

The following morning I received a message from our office that my friend Loraine in Hawaii wanted to tell me urgently about a most extraordinary experience she had had while swimming with the dolphins on the big island of Hawaii. I was able to get in touch with her and was glad that I did. She was still excited about her experience and had wanted to call me because she felt that there may be a deeper meaning in it for me too.

While swimming in a bay on the big island that is frequented by spinner dolphins for resting, playing, and mating, a group of dolphins had come very close to her and her friend. She noted that some swimmers in the bay did not know the dolphin-swim etiquette and often got left behind. They were so excited to finally see a dolphin that they dashed after them only to cause the dolphins to disappear. Learning to swim with dolphins usually requires some education. I knew how hard it was just to control all the new gear, negotiate the deep water, and then be sensitive enough to feel what is appropriate behavior. I have found that imagery is one of the most effective tools to be successful in swimming with wild dolphins.

Today Loraine had received an amazing communication while swimming in the bay with them.

Just as she was swimming back to shore with her friend, she started hearing the dolphins' sonar behind her in a peculiar way. She felt as if they were trying to get something across to her. The swimming had been fabulous. Earlier a group of dolphins had been spinning around her in a circle, like a whirlpool, receding down to a narrow point, taking her into the middle while keeping eye contact with her. Then she was on the way back and felt like she should have understood something, but she didn't know what it could be.

Suddenly she saw a school of goatfish sideways underneath her, a highly unusual sight in this bay. This school of goatfish looked like an Etch-a-Sketch and with a sudden understanding she knew that the dolphins were going to communicate with her through this underwater living chalkboard.

"Can you imagine?" she shared with a voice full of joy. "First I saw these geometric-like figures being sketched out in the living body of the goatfish. I don't know how they did it, but the images reminded me of the kind of geometric figures that are created by laying sand on a drum or a thin skin of some sort, and then stimulating it with sounds, each sound creating a different resonant image."

I had indeed seen such images and was intrigued by them. Sharry Edwards of Signature Sound Works in Athens, Ohio, has studied sound extensively and discovered that human health is related to the kind of sounds that are, or are not, present in a person's voice. She has mapped human voices and discovered that when certain notes found in the chromatic music scale are missing or stressed, this corresponds with a certain disease pattern. Conversely, she has found that if people play, sing, or somehow otherwise reintroduce the missing or stressed sounds into their human system, they will heal. Miracles have happened as a result of reintroducing the missing sound.

At one particular Global Science Congress, where Don and I had given a lecture, Ms. Edwards gave a multimedia presentation about her work. It was truly amazing. We saw video footage of a patient who had been paralyzed able to move his arm again after sound therapy!

For me the most amazing slides were the ones in which Ms. Edwards had imaged the shape of a mosque while singing a pure note. A sensitive spectrum analyzer had registered the sound of her voice and printed a computer analysis of the frequency image on paper. To everyone's surprise, it looked like an image of a mosque with a bell-shaped roof, the kind that comes together at a point. Another image she projected was that of a bell, with the same results. The shape of the image she held in her mind while singing seemed to be transportable to paper through analysis of the sound frequencies.

"Maybe we should all be more discerning about the images we carry in our minds," I thought.

Loraine continued her story. The most amazing image she saw in the school of goatfish was that of a "doughnut-like shape." "It was the closest image I knew from my human life that made sense," she said. I laughed and asked her if she thought the dolphins were trying to tell her to go to shore and eat a healthy doughnut.

"No, not that," she responded. "It felt more cosmic, but I couldn't make out what it was supposed to mean. Honestly, I called because I thought you could help me," she finished.

Then it dawned on me! The doughnut shape! A toroid! The image of the matrix of creation! The dolphins may have signaled the image of creation to her, sketching the image into the willing school of goat fish.

In the dream I had the night before Morey B. King talked about the flatlanders, I had been given the image of the matrix of creation, the toroid. Ever since then the image had haunted me, and I had begun to understand how the imagery work our Time Traveler taught us followed the matrix of the toroid.

Black holes transform into white holes. In the imagery transformation process we talk to an old image, one which is often full of pain or otherwise stopping the flow of life. We then follow it to its deepest core, into the black hole, so to speak, only to discover that beyond this lies yet a deeper desire that can be likened to a white hole, its true intent. When this underlying intent expresses itself and becomes its new image, it is much like crossing from the regions of the black hole through to the white hole. By doing this we shift dimensions. We recycle the previous energy and take it to a new level.

I had come to accept that, here at this level of manifestation, with each new thought we set an action into motion that will eventually "cool" down, become manifest, and eventually become a black hole, the stepping stone for the next frequency shift to yet a higher form of expression of life.

Life doesn't seem to stop when it reaches the "top" of Oneness, the ultimate union with God. From what I could comprehend of my dream experience, albeit a limited view, life continuously goes on. To me the refuge in all matters of creation is *to be centered in God awareness* in Oneness as often as possible *while living in creation*. I saw myself at the center of the toroid where life collapses into the black hole and then expands back out into the white hole, as well as on the periphery. The toroid looked like a cascading fountain, showering back onto itself, moving up through the center, entering again the Center, Oneness, Home.

In order to rise above the turmoil of the fluctuation of darkness and light, one has to be able to encompass both polarities. This is one of the secrets of the universe. Once one is able to contain a paradox within oneself, one automatically is "beyond" it, free of the oscillation between one or the other.

Learning to love and appreciate the old and often destructive feelings and images within ourselves, we are free to let the deeper and higher potential come to life. But first we must be able to hold both within our hearts.

The toroid is a *symbolic* expression of how the universe functions, and many seers, visionaries, and people who have had near-death experiences have seen the same vision. Loraine had not yet stumbled across the information about the toroid and was enthralled by the meaning of it. The toroid is like an infinity loop, only more complex, and it encompasses not only the idea of eternal reality and infinity, but many more aspects such as "becoming and un-becoming," "dark and light," 'multiple dimensions," "Oneness and multiplicity," "God and Creation" as ongoing dichotomy.

Was I helping Loraine understand the message the dolphins possibly had sent her, or was I supposed to understand something more? I certainly felt like the doughnut message was a deep reaffirmation of my own inner observations. I felt in tune with the imagery work we had been studying. Was there more?

45

The trip to Key West had been very satisfying, and I felt deeply grateful to Roberta for having shared this opportunity with us. Filled with new experiences and heightened in our sense of awe for the dolphins, we returned home. Our office needed attention, as work had piled up while we were gone. My flute also had been calling me, and I had missed playing it while traveling so much.

Our recordings were going well, and I discovered new levels of sounds resonating from within myself. Each change I went through in one area of my life deepened my abilities in all others, which I could clearly hear in my music now. Sometimes I sat down with my flute and traveled in my mind while I played. I tapped into such a mysterious place and let it teach me. It was a future place where I was in perfect harmony with the music and my flute. In the weeks to come I would notice with joy how much I was growing. I let my future teach me.

One day, as we were in the middle of things to do and projects to finish, we got a call from our inventor friend Eldon Byrd, the one who had taught us how to bend spoons. He had been invited to speak at a conference in Mexico about his dolphin research. He called to see if we might want to go to the conference that fall. *Dolphin-assisted therapy* was the theme.

We had originally met Eldon at a USPA Conference (United States Psychotronic Association) where he, Don, and I each gave lectures on different topics. His topic had been about dolphin sounds and his discoveries. One thing that stood out in my memory about his research was the following.

When dolphins were present in open waters and no human had yet entered the water, there was no sign of a sixteen-hertz signal coming from the dolphins. This frequency represents the more busy, mental frequency that human brains usually produce during waking hours. When humans entered the water, suddenly the sixteen-hertz signal would be generated by the dolphins. If a person enters into an imagery or meditative state, the brain frequencies drop down between eight and ten hertz. Sleep is associated with one to four hertz. Dolphins seem to be able to pick up the human range of frequencies and then send them back, possibly in an attempt to establish contact.

Eldon was calling to see if we wanted to come along to the conference. It surely would fit into our quest to gain more understanding about dolphins. The conference was going to be held in Cancun, Mexico, and was rather inexpensive. We checked our schedule, realized that we could easily take that week off, and made travel arrangements right away.

While we were waiting in San Jose for our connecting flight to Mexico, I was drawn to a copy of Time magazine, that faced us squarely from a newsstand. The article nearly floored me.

The president of France was insisting on staying on schedule with his planned nuclear testing in the South Pacific, despite worldwide resistance and reprimands! Not just one detonation was planned, but six altogether. Nothing, and he said *nothing*, would make him change his mind!

Since I normally don't read the newspaper, nor do I have a television on which to watch the news, the information on the planned nuclear tests had totally evaded me.

Reading the headlines at the airport I suddenly got the big picture. As if struck by lightening, I understood the dolphin message I received several months earlier when we were swimming in Key West. The underwater detonation, the shape of an exploding bomb I saw when I asked how I could help the dolphins, all started making sense now. But what could I do?

I was not aware of the political frenzy that had gone on for months already, with actions by Greenpeace demonstrating against the nuclear testing.

The dolphins in the waters off Key West must have known of the plight that would face marine inhabitants in months to come. Something big was up in the world of the dolphins' World Wide Web. Did they know of the coming event, an event that was to happen in the future? I had not known anything about this, but they obviously did.

I felt at a loss. This task of helping them with the underwater testing seemed way too big. What could I do anyway? I did decide to support Greenpeace monthly since I could see the urgent need for funds in cases like this, but what else could be done?

This question stayed with me for another few weeks until an idea dawned on me. It was something the dolphins seemed to have pointed out in my life throughout all these years. But first we were to attend the dolphin conference.

46

The conference was very well organized, and we were met at the airport's exit. Cancun is a city that has been built for tourists, and it holds little of the old Mexico we had hoped for. On the other hand, we were treated to luxurious rooms and pools and ocean waters at very low prices, and I decided not to resist what was in front of me.

The conference began with a cocktail evening for everyone to get to know each other. The conference theme was dolphin-assisted therapy, and it became clear in a short time that most of the people who would present papers were working with captive dolphins. Within a couple of hours a small group of people had clustered together who were involved in open-water research with wild dolphins. I found out that there was a big rift in the dolphin community between wild- and captive-dolphin proponents. The reason more wild-dolphin researchers were not present was because they had not been invited. Since like attracts like, I could understand why.

In our little group of "wild-dolphin contact proponents" were Kim from Denmark, who did dolphin research in Israel and was at the conference to report on it for a film network in Denmark; Eldon, who had done his research in the open waters on dolphin sound frequencies that went outside the range previously measured by the navy; Terry, a lady from Oahu who helps people connect with wild dolphins; Scott from Colorado, who took people into the ocean to swim with dolphins; and Don and me.

The next day was filled with reports from trainers, therapists, and researchers who had worked with humans and captive dolphins in an attempt to find out and define the benefits humans derive from swimming with dolphins. They told of autistic children who broke out of their isolation around dolphins, some speaking their first words; of children who were behaviorally impaired and who seemed to improve in and out of the water when near dolphins; of depressed people who felt jubilant around dolphins; and of adults in chronic pain who temporarily lost their pain after swimming with dolphins.

From all the presentations filled with slides and detailed information, it became evident that dolphins have an amazing knack for healing. Humans seem to benefit from being in the water with them and dolphin-assisted therapy is being considered as a reputable therapy for humans.

One of the most far-out concepts concerned hooking up dolphins to wires in a virtual-reality setting in order to transmit dolphin-contact experiences to people who cannot, for reasons of immobility or severe illness, undergo the actual experience. I raised my hand and said, "If I understand this correctly, we humans are looking to harness the healing powers of captive dolphins through technology and use these powers on humans who are sick *because of* technology and its toxic waste so they can experience temporary relief."

I guess they didn't like my observation since they brushed over it quickly, but the concept I saw at work baffled me. Is it right for humans to use other beings for our benefit without their consent? To my knowledge, dolphins have yet to voluntarily enter the lagoons or tanks in any captive situation.

I can certainly understand that there is a vast diversity of thought on our planet. We can't even agree on a common concept of God, let alone ethics, and we tend to see humankind as the crowning achievement of creation, according ourselves the "right" to decide the fate of others. In the Western world we have fallen a long way from thinking seven generations deep and loving the earth we walk on. Which way is right?

All I could do was decide with whom I was going to align my energy, which way of communing with dolphins I was going to choose. The following day made my choice easy. In my heart, though, I honored everyone's effort and desire to help people. Who knows? It might be through dolphin-assisted therapy that dolphins get enough public attention to ensure clean oceans and continued survival of this splendid species with their wonderfully developed brains.

The next day we were all invited to a swim with captive dolphins in a lagoon. The owners of the dolphinarium were gracious, and I felt quite honored to be there. We would be divided into two groups of six people, each group having two dolphins with which to be. The time in the water was divided into trained behavior, like being pushed through the water with a dolphin's nose against our feet, jumping over a stick we would hold in the air, or swimming past our outstretched hands, so that we could pet them. It was the first time I had touched a dolphin and I almost cried, because it was obvious to me that one of the dolphins did not want to be touched, yet had to do the trick anyway as best as it could in order to get fed its meal of fish. In some show situations, withholding of food is a means by which dolphin trainers enforce "desired" behaviors.

A dolphin's skin is very sensitive and feels absolutely smooth. They actually love physical contact, especially among themselves in the ocean, and we have seen them rub each other often in the open waters.

Their "trained" behavior felt like a circus act, but I guess it is a tangible way for humans to grasp that contact with dolphins *is* happening, since many of the subtleties of their behavior may be beyond the human capacity of perception.

At the end we were given a ten- to fifteen-minute period of swimming freely among the dolphins. We were twelve people, and the four dolphins who got fed for swimming back and forth kept passing us in the water. The people who had learned to dive and hold their breath were getting a lot more out of the swimming time. Don and I tried our telepathic communication. Don imaged a big bright ball of light in the water and asked the dolphins to indicate that they could see his projection by swimming right through the ball of light.

The first time a dolphin swam through this imagined ball of light, Don couldn't believe it and thought it might just have been coincidence. He placed the imagined ball at a different location, now farther away from any swimming patterns that might account for a "coincidental" passing through. But to Don's surprise a dolphin came zooming right through the middle of his light ball. Again and again he tried, and the results were always the same.

In another part of the lagoon I was enjoying diving and swirling in a circle with one of the dolphins. He kept eye contact with me, and I wondered what he might want me to write in my book about dolphins. At one point I said in my mind, "If you can understand me, please come over to me." I really didn't say words in my mind but rather saw a feeling-image tied together as a ball of information. The dolphin came face to face with me and almost stood still in front of me. I had not seen this behavior before, since dolphins rarely swim head on toward someone, and certainly not without promising them food, or unless it's a trainer.

I was startled when suddenly a dolphin "stood" in exactly the same position as I had imagined, confirming that at least the dolphins could understand us accurately.

"Yes, what do you want to communicate?" I heard next. Dumbfounded, I asked what he/she might want me to write about in my book on dolphins. Instantaneously, information was telepathically downloaded. I feel frustrated sometimes, as I believe they can give us so much information, but our capacity for understanding life, and our knowledge about time and space are still so limited that we can't fully understand the dolphins. Many times when swimming with them I have been unable to grasp what was being communicated. But I know that *they* can hear us pretty clearly.

The fifteen minutes of swimming time passed way too quickly, and we got out of the water to let the next group of twelve people have their turn. Don was depressed about the dolphin's situation. Most of the others had had no prior experience of meeting dolphins, but Don had. The level of presence and intensity we experienced from the dolphins was drastically different from what we experience when meeting wild dolphins in the open ocean. We figured that because these dolphins were in a captive situation they had "toned themselves down" in order to live in their confined condition. I have rarely seen Don depressed but this experience really got to him.

Some people had the best time of their life, and I was smiling for them, too. But in my heart I could not see myself ever coming back here.

We asked the trainers what they had observed about dolphins being telepathic and whether they had ever practiced communicating this way. It seemed to happen only rarely that trainers realized a telepathic link existed, and they still wondered how the dolphin could have known what was wanted of them. We also asked the trainers who worked for dolphin-assisted therapy programs, but they told us they were so busy training specific behaviors that they hadn't noticed anything else.

Needless to say, there are many different degrees of awareness in humans, as there are in dolphins. Many people do not know that telepathy is something we all do, since it happens mostly unconsciously, and we are taught in the west that it is at best a childhood fantasy.

The conference was over, and a call for volunteers went out to help organize next year's event. I was not willing to support captive dolphins in order to help humans. If the dolphins could freely choose whether to swim around humans or not, that would be another matter.

By now I was also understanding how well dolphins can connect with humans out of the water. My dolphin dreams certainly have been amazing highlights in my life. As I take my inner life more seriously, it becomes more real.

This trip had been worthwhile, though, as Don and I returned home with a deeper understanding of dolphins. My love and respect for these amazing beings had grown even more, and I was now beginning to wonder how high the dolphins' level of consciousness actually was. Their request for help with the nuclear testing still puzzled me.

47

Fall was well in progress when we arrived back home from the conference. The difference between the hot climate in Mexico and the cool temperatures on our island in the Pacific Northwest made the crisp smells of autumn even more noticeable. I loved to take walks in the forest near the cliffs of the island.

One late afternoon a blend of pine and madrona trees whose bare silken trunks were bathed in the orange glow of the evening's setting sun, greeted me as I meandered down the narrow path. It made my heart sing. The earth smelled moist, and the sun created long shadows on the rich forest floor. As I saw my shadow touch the ground where the sun shone through the trees I felt ancient. This could be a moment in the long-distant past. This shadow could be that of an American Indian who harvested the berries and mushrooms in these forests, who fished in the ocean below, and who gazed at the eagles as they flew overhead.

A sudden stirring brought me out of the past as I saw an eagle lift swiftly from a tree nearby. "What amazing timing," I marveled. This could also be sometime in the future. How would life be then? *What had we as the human race done to create a future in which paradise was a reality?*

The answer dawned on me. People will have realized the power of their dreams. Not only the dreams of the few who paved the way for things to come important, but the dreams of each and every individual also were shaping the fabric of life. At first a few, then more and more people realized the power of their imagination. Had it not been the trees in this forest who told me that our human potential lay in the power of us dreaming reality into being?

A more pressing question surfaced within me. "How can I contribute, especially in regard to the dolphin's request for help with underwater nuclear testing?" I wondered.

I suddenly got the obvious answer! I could re-dream the fabric in my own universe. I settled on the high banks of the bluff overlooking the waters below me. Glistening sunlight reflected from the water, and a million starbursts of light were dancing on the waves.

In my mind's eye I rose into the world of vision. I loved to go to the place where I saw the gridwork of light lines over our planet. There, every single light represents an idea and is in instantaneous contact with the information surrounding the entire planet. There, I meet like-minded "workers" in the light grid.

The French minister was the leadership voice for the choices that had been made about the nuclear testing. Much like I had connected with the "head" energy in a pod of dolphins, I now made contact with this being who was heading France. I love France. I love to speak French and felt for the poor image France was creating in the eyes of the entire planet.

At the level of seeing the original energy patterns, I asked what that decision was about and asked about the feelings of hardness that accompanied the decision. Whether the answers I received were accurate in relation to real life I do not know, but I sensed that the cause came from a hardened heart, one that had covered up the need for love and settled instead for toughness and power.

I asked this energy being, which I imagined to be the French president, what this hardness really wanted. As it revealed to me the president's depth of aloneness, even in the relationships with his loved ones, it let me see the desire for love. I asked this hardness what it would look like if it had the love it really wanted. The answer I saw was the image of a ring of daisies, symbolizing the love and warmth that would heal his soul.

I invited him to hug the old hard feeling that had been in his heart and then asked him to let the old image become part of the new one. The hardness gave way and turned into the ring of daisies. It became love and respect, especially from the ones closest to him, as well as from those in the world at large. I was moved. Could I ever have suspected that hardness of heart could lead a politician to make choices that would affect the entire world?

In the imaginary transformation in my mind, I saw the ripple effect this new image and feeling would have around the planet, and I thanked it deeply. Then I let go.

I turned my attention to the trees around me and to the orange-red sun about to set. The air had cooled down considerably, and I was getting chilly. For some reason I loved this feeling of cooling down with the sunset, feeling the evening dusk slowly cover the earth with its blanket of the coming night.

I sent gratitude out to the sun for having warmed us and

for sending us light. I wondered about the tales of the "first people," who say that they still greet the sun in the morning and evening, and should they ever not be here to do this ritual and no one else takes their place, they are sure that this will signal the end of the world.

Maybe it is time for us in the West to remember the knowledge we have from when we were the "first people." We need to remember the ancient wisdom of interconnecting life with our dreaming mind and with our consciousness. We all once lived in such a way that we dreamed the day into being, and some people are starting to remember now.

I got up from the prickly ground I had been sitting on and made my way home. Walking in a state of reverie, I gazed at the trees and hoped that my dreaming was making it possible for future generations of radiant men and women to enjoy the wisdom and comfort of trees.

Then I went home to Don.

48

As I entered the door Don came bouncing down the hallway to hug me. I loved how we often greeted each other as if it were the first time. Happy to see me, he looked into my eyes, smiling warmly. Within the blue ocean of light in his eyes I saw the one Source, and we touched in our souls, surrendering our spirits into One. If I were to draw a picture, it would look like two radiant rays converging. At the moment they touch and unify, a grand opening of the lights of Heaven would wrap itself around us, taking us beyond the sense of self into the vistas of Love, God and Bliss.

"It is through this union that we do all our work and share our gifts with the world," I realized, and I felt a deep desire to help more and more people find their highest expression of the dreams within them.

Imagery is one of the key elements propelling us along the path of enlightening our inner and outer world. With our focus on the Source, imagery has been the secret key. With its help we have entered worlds of mystery, miracles, love, and the magic of creating. We have been able to give to the world because we have learned how to make our dreams come true. We have written and published books and music, taught seminars, and work internationally in numerous countries. Through the use of imagery millions of people can become aligned with their highest purpose and dreams, and live a life that rewards them with the pleasures of deep gratitude. They can feel thankful and joyous to be alive.

Dolphins and the Time Traveler have opened the way for me, and I am happy to be a creative energy within the matrix of God's creation. I will do my best to let more people know of the possibilities that lie waiting within each person's heart.

I remembered the struggle at first when I was worried about being "trapped" in the web of illusion and smiled about my journey through the many questions I had had over the years. Looking back I saw that there is no other place to be other than in the hands of God.

Life works because it is designed to work. It either works slowly and painfully while we resist it, or it works effortlessly while we cooperate with it. In either case, we learn the lessons of Love and Life.

To cooperate with life, I have had to learn to open continuously to the higher forces and let invisible hands help me. I have had to let go of emotions and habits that kept reinforcing the same unproductive patterns, face my fears, allow them to become my allies, and dive deeper to look for the underlying intent of any such patterns, which turned out to be my very own potential.

Life is created twice, once as a potential and then in form in the many manifested dimensions. Our inner images serve as a flashlight illuminating the one choice we make from the many potentials that exist in the body of God. Each experience is valid; it's just that some seem to be endowed with life-giving energy while others seem to reduce this feeling. Luckily, we as living organisms are coded with an eventual preference for energy and experiences that give life, although some take a long time to discover this. Sooner or later all creation has the drive to return to the Source.

Ilona Selke

49

Months passed in a flurry of activities. Seminars, publishing books and recording music filled our days. We kept teaching seminars to other people who wanted to teach the methods of imagery we had learned. The "Living From Vision" course had been taught in Germany for some time, and one day we received a bundle of notes one teacher had saved from all the different participants who had described their journeys through this course. Don and I poured over the letters with great joy, and tears ran down our faces. I felt grateful to be part of people's growth. It was deeply satisfying beyond words.

The winter months were cool, and we stayed close to the fireside. The shortest days crowned the middle of winter, heralding the longer days of spring that I looked forward to with delightful anticipation. It was sometime early in the new year that I received a phone call from Greenpeace.

"Hi, this is Ilona at Living from Vision; can I help you?" I asked.

"Yes," the voice of a woman answered. "We are calling to update you on some vital information and want to get your support. First of all, we want to inform you that the French president has withdrawn his intent to detonate all of the scheduled nuclear bombs except the first one! He is insisting that it had nothing to do with Greenpeace's effort, but we are delighted no matter what the cause." She was happy to have brought me good news. "We thought you might like to hear the great news and at the same time would like to ask you to consider becoming a monthly supporting member."

I was floored, barely able to tell her that I was already a monthly supporting member. "Oh, I am sorry," the friendly Greenpeace voice replied. "We shouldn't have bothered you. You accidentally wound up on this list."

"Oh, don't be sorry; I am delighted to hear the good news. Thank you for informing me," I responded, then hung up the phone.

Stunned, I felt like the world around me stood still. What was going on in this universe? I remembered the dolphin's request for help with the underwater testing of nuclear bombs, and I recalled my imaginary session in the forest overlooking the water. In the months that had gone by, I had not thought much about it and had not checked the news to see what was happening. Only occasionally had I sent love to the ring of daisies, knowing they were at work in my version of the universe.

If Greenpeace had not called, I don't know when I would have learned about the cancellation of the testing. I was happy for the world, happy for the dolphins, happy for France. I was overwhelmed by the implications, at least as far as I understood them, for imagery.

Granted, I could not say that the changes happened as a result of my imagery, but who cared. I now lived in a world that was in harmony with what I was able to hold in my heart. Love, understanding, and embracing seemed to be the answer, and the world I lived in reflected my inner changes. Maybe we all dream our own world into existence.

Maybe there are as many possibilities outside us as there are inside, and if so, I can make my choice by focusing on and understanding the reality and potential I am able to live.

I jumped into the air and ran to see Don. "Don, guess what? France dropped their insistence on detonating the underwater nuclear bombs!" I almost sang. We hugged, cried, and held each other.

"A lot of other beings are happy too, I'm sure," whispered Don.

We winked at each other. "Welcome to Heaven on Earth."

Epilogue

The vision of what is possible for humanity is staggering. We are not peons in a grand and senseless game of Life, but rather co-creative sparks of consciousness, co-dreamers in the dream of God.

Today we are at a crossroads where it looks like humanity may be in a swamp of turmoil, not knowing which way to turn. But hidden within our core lies the seed of the same energy that constitutes all of creation, God. If we listen to the subtle whisperings of our innermost voices, we will find a path through the seemingly unsurveyed chaos in which we find ourselves.

By traversing the inner realms of potential through imagery and transformational processes, we can discover the purpose of our life, transform our dark spots, and then dream a promising dream for our future, one in which our children will be grateful to live.

As we learn to discover more of who we are, our conscious dreaming will send ripples through entire worlds of creation. At first we may feel like a pebble dropped into a vast blue lake, and our dreams may seem like a single stone causing only a tiny ripple in the water. Quickly however, another, grander ring will follow until we discover that all the ripples that were sent forth by the single stone have encompassed the entire lake.

Our sense of "self" is only limited by the size of what we believe we are, because in truth we are all of creation.

The innermost potential, the inner guiding and radiant voices, can be accessed through the methods I have outlined in this book. For those of you who want to delve deeper into the workings of these methods, you may contact us, and learn more deeply how to transform your life into one of brilliance and light.

Some of you may want to teach these methods and we can assist in that as well. Some of you are or will be inner guardians who in your dreaming will create parts of a new tomorrow.

Just as dolphins can be thought of as one "unit," so can humanity. We can ask for the deepest desire and truest intent of this "entity" called humanity to reveal itself. As we carry this new image on the radio station of our own mind, we will set up a resonance with the entire lake, provided we have accessed a true higher potential. Our vision will resonate with the lake because it is true, because there is no doubting the potential that lives within ourselves. It simply is and wants to come alive.

What I love most about the imagery transformation process I described in the book, is the fact that, although the changes can be staggeringly powerful, we at no time have power "over" anything. In the imagery process we simply uncover the hidden potential lying dormant within any problem or blockage. In no case do we ever impose our own wishes upon anything. We simply ask the energy in question, no matter how convoluted it may look, what it truly wants. We simply discover and then hold the vision of its inherent potential. Even when the vision of the potential is only half of the story, it soon will blossom like a flower in a garden we have tended.

Wisdom of the Dolphins

As humans, we need to tend the garden of our dreams and visions well, and we will be rewarded with and will embody the fruits of our care. Remember that we are all imbued with the same seed dream of God. All we need to do is hone ourselves back to the Source, the core.

I hope I have given some of you a vision of what is possible, a vision the dolphins have shared with me.

The first time our Time Traveler transformed a global vision (the orange gas cloud that turned into peace games), he found the astounding confirmation that his imagery transformation had taken hold in the physical world when he and the man from the pentagon met while swimming with dolphins.

Both the Time Traveler and I had similar experiences in imagery work when we entered the world of dolphins. Just maybe, the dolphins know how to shape-shift through the universe and are willing to help any human who is willing to listen and learn to do the same.

I have found that it is not necessary to swim physically with dolphins in order to have a connection with them. Dolphins are adept at inter-dimensional communication and sharing. All you need to do is focus your soul's intention in harmony with the dolphins, and they will connect with you.

May we all learn to live together in gratitude and joy in this bubble of creation, and may we all be touched by the grace of God.

Contact

Ilona Selke

Information about Ilona Selke:
http://www.ilonaselke.com

E-Mail:
info@ilonaselke.com

Order online at
www.ilonaselke.com
or call:
1-800-758-7836 / 1-360-387-5713
Books:

Dolphins, Love and Destiny

Alin Learns to Use His Imagination

Video:
Living From Vision Course

Living From Vision® is a miraculous Online or Home Study DVD course to help you feel powerful and manifest your greatest dreams so you can live happily and fulfill your purpose in life.

Life is about developing depth of soul; it's about understanding the laws of the universe, the 101 of creation. It's about learning to love and co-create reality.

If you want to develop your power to create, to live in harmony with your intuition, and explore your life form the inside out, then THIS is the course for you! If you have seen or read The Secret, this course will allow you to put the Secret to work in your own life. Imagine that you are one of the people in the Secret telling their success story. This is the power of Living From Vision.

This course Living From Vision® teaches whole brain thinking, imagery, relaxed focusing and immediate action.
No matter how many trainings you have taken, this course will give you wings. "It is a grand recipe that actually works!" (quoted by students world wide)

This course really delivers! A structured five-week course leads you to actually live what you truly envision. By dealing clearly with the feedback you encounter as your actions begin to manifest, obstacles are easily resolved, and the natural flow of creation comes through you.
This is a powerful course for anyone who wants more from their life, and is willing to commit to a process of creating it.

You will practice:
- How to manifest your visions, goals, wishes
- How to find and express your personal purpose
- Step-by-step methods to ensure your goals come to life
- How to make negative emotions work for you
- Ways to handle stress effectively
- How to create a happy life, & sit in the driver's seat of your life
- Develop your creativity.... yes, ... write, sing, travel....
- Have the financial dreams of yours come true
- Develop your emotional and intuitive IQ
- Have time for yourself again   ... b r e a t h e ...
- Make the special projects you've dreamed about come true
- Face your fears.... turn them around to become your allies
- Feel empowered
- Develop a higher version of YOU and live it

New! Now available as an online course.

Now you can download the Living From Vision course and immediately begin learning how to now create the life you want to live! You will get an online day-planner that incorporates the Living From Vision principles and daily audio exercises, as well as a Daily Diary that is searchable by key words. It can also be used as a Dream Diary to keep track of your important dreams and search for common themes in your nightly adventures.

Music:

Himalayan Soul

Romantic Wonder

Mind Journey Music

Inner Spheres

In One We Are

Yoga with Ilona

DVD and CD set

This series of easy Yoga exercises will transform you body gently and easily with daily practice. Learn the positions and the flow of the asanas (positions) by following with the DVD.

After you have mastered the progression of the exercises (usually within a week), you can use the provided CD and listen to Ilona guide you through your morning routine with some beautiful background music from Inner Spheres.

Guided Meditation CDs

1. Mission in Life / Healing your Body
2. Time Travel / Abundance
3. Spiritual Partnership / Dreamtime Awakening
4. Healing the Earth / Dolphin Consciousness

To order please visit www.ilonaselke.com
or call toll free:
1-800-758-7836
or
1-360-387-5713

ShangriLa Oceanside Wellness Center

www.bali-shangrila.com

Explore the magic of the north shore of Bali as you treat yourself to wellness and adventure at our SHANGRI LA Wellness Resort.

Enjoy a week or a weekend of Wellness Treatments, Yoga, Meditation, Snorkeling, Dolphin Watching and gourmet vegetarian meals (fish optional).

We are nestled next to a traditional fishermen's village, where you can explore Bali as only few will know it. You can enjoy safe swimming and snorkeling in the beauty of our corral reef preserve which is located right in front of your villa.

On early mornings you can take excursions on an outrigger boat with one of the fishermen to watch dolphins, or enjoy the sunrise and the stunning view of the mountains on the north coast of Bali.

Our beautiful resort, with it's loving staff and well trained therapists, will treat you to a wellness experience that will stay in your memory for ever.

We are located 1 3/4 hours from Ubud right on the beach.
Call our manager Made for directions or to arrange transportation.
+62 81 338 674 895

ShangriLa Oceanside Retreat and Spa
+62 362-28351
Bondalem, Bali

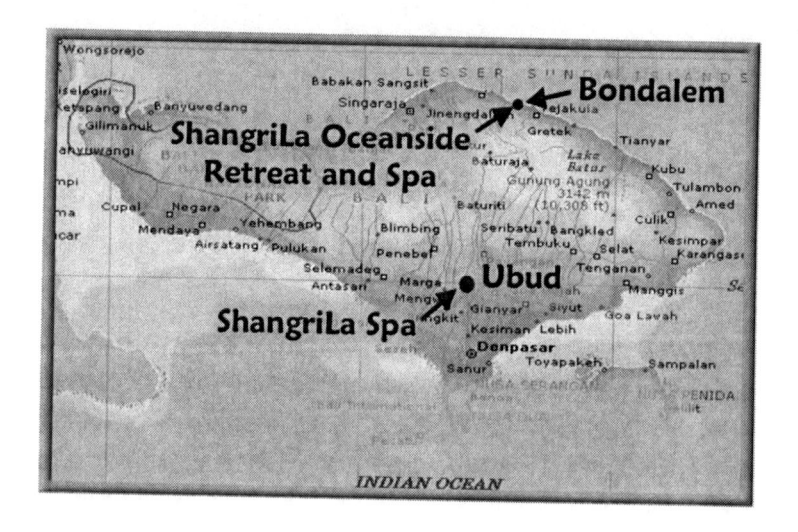

ShangriLa Spa on Lotus Lane

Discover the Mystery

- **M**assage
- **A**ccupressure
- **S**ound Healing
- **R**eflexology

www.ubudmassage.com

- **M**anicure
- **P**edicure
- **F**acial

On Monkey Forest Rd.
Ubud, Bali

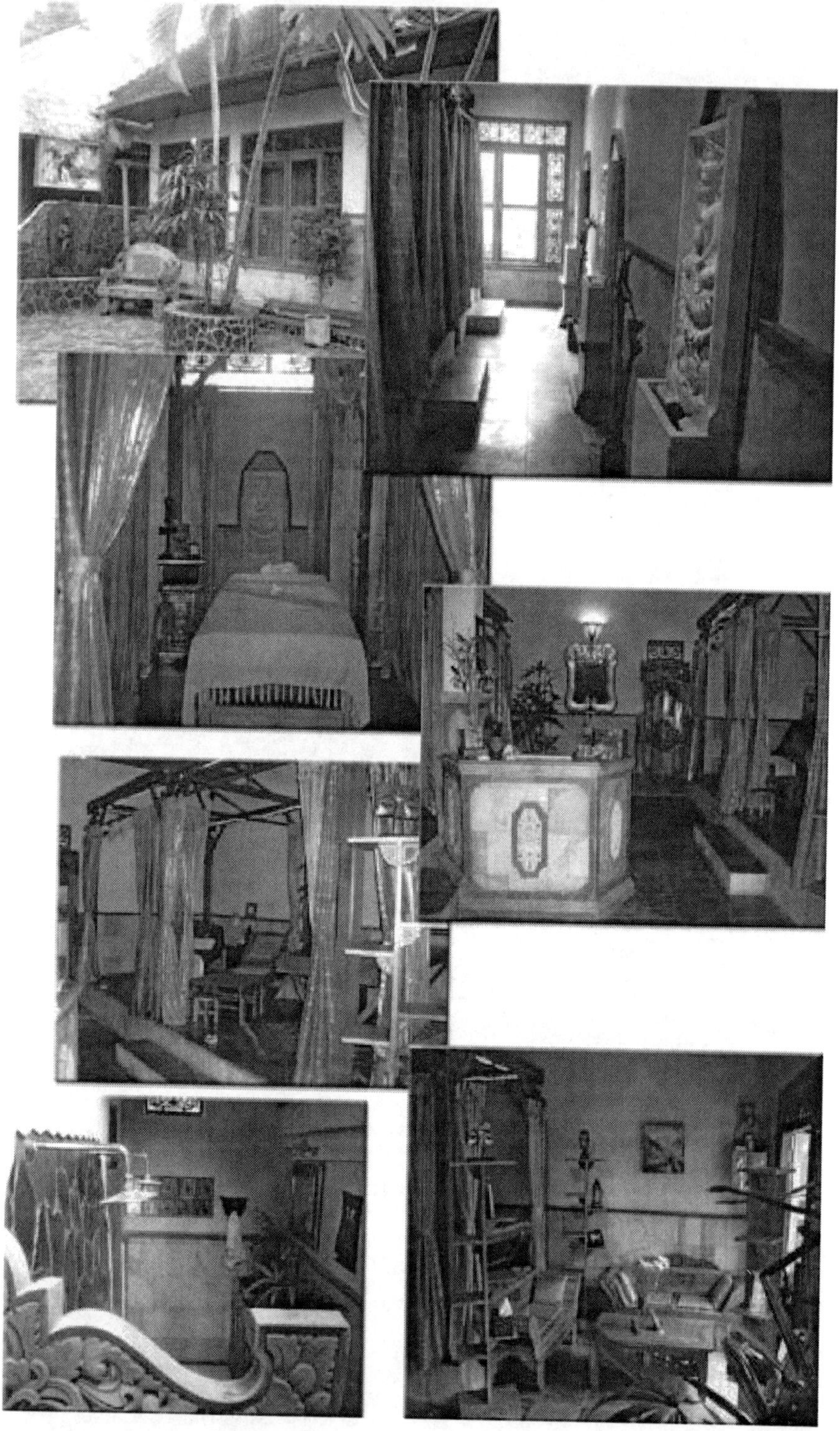

ShangriLa Spa

Discover the Mystery

- Ubud Market
- Soccer Field
- Cafe Wyan
- Shangrila Spa
- Lotus Lane Restaurant
- Lotus Lane
- Monkey Forest Rd.
- Hanuman Rd.
- Dirty Duck

0361-919-2547
www.Ubudmassage.com